Collins

Key Stage 3
Geographical
Enquiry
Teacher Book 1

David Weatherly
Nicholas Sheehan
Rebecca Kitchen

William Collins' dream of knowledge for all began with the publication of his first book in 1819. A self-educated mill worker, he not only enriched millions of lives, but also founded a flourishing publishing house. Today, staying true to this spirit, Collins books are packed with inspiration, innovation and practical expertise. They place you at the centre of a world of possibility and give you exactly what you need to explore it.

Collins. Freedom to teach

Published by Collins
An imprint of HarperCollins Publishers Ltd
Westerhill Road
Bishopbriggs
Glasgow G64 2QT
www.harpercollins.co.uk

Collins® is a registered trademark of HarperCollins Publishers Ltd

**Browse the complete Collins catalogue at
www.collins.co.uk**

First edition 2014

© HarperCollins Publishers Limited 2014

Maps © Collins Bartholomew Ltd 2014

10 9 8 7

ISBN 978-0-00-741115-3

David Weatherly, Nicholas Sheehan and Rebecca Kitchen assert their moral rights to be identified as the authors of this work.

A catalogue record for this book is available from the British Library

Typeset and designed by Mark Walker Design
Cover and title page designs by Angela English

Printed and bound by CPI Group (UK) Ltd, Croydon CR0 4YY

Most of the mapping in this publication is generated from Collins Bartholomew digital databases.
Collins Bartholomew, the UK's leading independent geographical information supplier, can provide a digital, custom, and premium mapping service to a variety of markets.
For further information:
Tel: +44 (0)208 307 4515
e-mail: collinsbartholomew@harpercollins.co.uk

Visit our websites at: www.collins.co.uk or www.collinsbartholomew.com

Acknowledgments:
p20 © Rainer Lesniewski/Shutterstock.com; p42 © Hillel J. Hoffman/National Geographic Creative; p48, 49, 50, 51 © EM-DAT: The OFDA/CRED International Disaster Database/www.emdat.be, Université Catholique de Louvain, Brussels (Belgium); p58 © Carolyn Barry/National Geographic Creative; p59 © Bee Wilson/Telegraph Media Group Limited 2013; p60 © weebly.com

The material on page 72 was written by Richard King, Policy Research Adviser at Oxfam GB. This post appeared at www.theguardian.com/global-development/poverty-matters/2011/jun/01/global-food-crisis-changing-diets on 01/06/2011 and is reproduced with the permission of Oxfam GB, Oxfam House, John Smith Drive, Cowley, Oxford OX4 2JY, UK www.oxfam.org.uk.Oxfam does not necessarily endorse any text or activities that accompany the materials.

Contents

Introduction   4

Enquiry 1: Living in Japan   6
Why isn't Yuna able to play the sport she loves?

Enquiry 2: Holes in the landscape   16
Why should we be concerned about sinkholes?

Enquiry 3: Is fracking all that its cracked up to be?   26
Is fracking a sustainable solution to the UK's energy security challenge?

Enquiry 4: Almost Armageddon!   36
Why did the earth nearly die at the end of the Permian period?

Enquiry 5: Disasters and risky places   46
Are Haiti and the Philippines risky places to live?

Enquiry 6: Don't snatch!   56
How is so-called 'land grabbing' affecting Africa?

Enquiry 7: Olympic spirit   66
Where should the 2022 Winter Olympics be held?

Blank outline maps   76

KS3 Geographical Enquiry

This *Geographical Enquiry* programme offers you a new and exciting approach to engaging your Key Stage 3 students with twenty-first century geography. It is the antithesis of the traditional textbook based 'double-page spread' method of teaching geography, which too often offers students only a superficial and disjointed perspective of the subject. In contrast, the approach taken in this programme is to connect students with wide-ranging and stimulating geographical questions and associated data that enable them to consider the subject in greater depth. This series gives students the opportunity to see the world as geographers and enables them to achieve and perform highly through carefully planned progression and challenge.

The following five principles have guided the design and structure of each enquiry:

1 Understanding the importance of geography as a discipline that enables students to recognise, describe, explain and evaluate the interactions between people and environments and acknowledging the central role geography plays in supporting these students to become 'agents of change'.

2 Recognising what it means to get better at geography in terms of intellectual outcomes and building progression in these skills. Excelling as a 'geographer' as opposed to just being 'good at geography' requires not only knowing and understanding the physical and human processes which shape the world in which we live, but also being challenged to apply that knowledge and understanding to new situations and to think both conceptually and critically. The following progression in geographical outcomes underlies each of the enquiries:

> **Recognise – identify – respond and ask questions – contribute views and opinions – use basic vocabulary**
>
> ↓
>
> **Describe – observe – reason– select**
>
> ↓
>
> **Classify – categorise – sequence – order – compare and contrast – use appropriate vocabulary**
>
> ↓
>
> **Demonstrate informed understanding through explanation – communicate informed views and opinions using accurate and specialist vocabulary**
>
> ↓
>
> **Apply – prioritise – analyse – describe and explain links, patterns, processes and interrelationships – reach conclusions**
>
> ↓
>
> **Synthesise – make substantiated and informed judgements consistent with evidence**
>
> ↓
>
> **Evaluate – critique – predict – hypothesize**

3 Not confusing subject 'outputs' with subject 'outcomes'. Each of the enquiries has a suggested output of learning such as a PowerPoint presentation; the design of a website home-page; a piece of persuasive writing or physical model. These outputs are not ends in themselves but vehicles for demonstrating geographical outcomes. Their value lies in what they indicate about the breadth and depth of geographical learning which has taken place e.g. to be able to evaluate the viewpoints of different stakeholders regarding a contentious issue. Such an approach makes assessment more straightforward i.e. in this example is there evidence of both appraisal of different perspectives and a judgement?

4 Ensuring and supporting engagement through thinking very hard about the modern geographical issues, places, themes and interactions that are of most relevance to young geographers today. Every enquiry has been informed by the subject content and recommendations of the 2014 National Curriculum in the

mastering of locational and place knowledge and the areas of study recommended for both human and physical geography. Comprehensive cross-referencing with the subject content of the Key Stage 3 programmes of study are detailed separately in the relevant section for each enquiry of this book, which also includes the supporting learning resources referred to in the Student Book. Each enquiry is made up of one overarching investigative question and a series of sub-questions serving to structure learning and provide both continuity and progression. This ensures that students gain crucial subject knowledge and understanding of the topics and relationships that lie at the heart of modern twenty-first century geography.

5 Making *structured enquiry* with plenty of opportunities to *consolidate your thinking* and *apply your skills* the driver for developing learning and reflection. Each of the enquiries has been designed to balance the need to provide the student with the key information required to progress through the enquiry along with the need to encourage the learner to ask as many questions themselves as possible.

Key question led enquiry based learning

Application of intellectual and subject skills

- Discerning where the students are in their learning:
  What do they already know?
  What can they already do?
  What do they already feel?
  How do they already act and react?

- Identifying appropriate outcomes for this stage of learning in geography

- Generating questions:
  What do the students want to find out?
  What is most geographically relevant for them to find out?
  Overarching investigative question
  Sub-questions

- Investigating through enquiry
  primary and secondary data collection

- Application of intellectual skills and subject tools e.g. graphicacy, literacy and numeracy to present and interpret data, reach conclusions and evaluate and critique results

- Meaningful geographical learning

In addition to the wide-ranging learning support materials in this Teacher Book further resources are also available to download from www.collins.co.uk/KS3Geogtr1.
These resources consolidate and extend student learning and have been created both to ensure that teachers possess detailed contextual information for each enquiry and also to provide ideas and spark interest in pursuing related investigations.

Downloadable resources include:

- Engaging and inspiring **Story Maps** for each enquiry which cover the basic geographical concepts that students will encounter in the Student Book

- Extensive **image galleries** related to each investigation

- **Word and PDF files** of the Teacher Book that enable teachers to either use the enquiry plans directly or adapt them according to the needs of individual students and groups

The overriding principle, which has guided the design and structure of the enquiries and learning resources in this series, has been to support and encourage students to see the world through the eyes of geographers, not geography students. We are confident that students will recognise both the relevancy of investigating the modern world they live in and the value of the enquiry method of teaching which prepares them for adult life, encourages high achievement and supports further learning.

Why isn't Yuna able to play the sport she loves?

▶ Purpose ◀

This investigation is designed to enable pupils to explore the relationship between physical environment and human activity, and how the two interact to determine spatial patterns and influence human behaviour. In Japan, the geographical constraints imposed by a largely mountainous terrain can be limiting factors. Through the story of one young professional Japanese woman, pupils are introduced to the relief of Japan and the nature of high-density living in urban areas along its coastal plains. Because flat land is scarce it is very expensive and therefore leisure pursuits such as tennis and golf can become very exclusive. This is Yuna's problem; finding the price of the sport she loves prohibitive.

Through the interpretation of a range of sources of geographical information, provided in the Student Book and in the teacher support materials, together with additional research areas which are suggested, pupils come to understand how the geography of Japan influences the life that Yuna leads. A framework is provided through the teacher support materials for the pupils to plan (using a model), draft, peer assess, and finalise a piece of extended explanatory writing which demonstrates their understanding, and to reach conclusions consistent with the evidence. The enquiry is then extended to enable the pupils to reflect on how Japan is altering its physical geography by creating new landscapes and environments to serve as living space.

Through the case study of the construction of the new Kansai International Airport from reclaimed land in Osaka Bay, pupils are able to consider the views of local and regional stakeholders and to evaluate whether they feel the operators of the airport have addressed concerns adequately through its Environmental Management Plan.

Finally, pupils are encouraged to consider the issue of how best to meet the need for increased airport capacity in Southeast England and to present the costs and benefits of the three live options, one of which is to build a new airport on reclaimed land in the Thames Estuary based on the Japanese model.

▶ Aims ◀

Through this enquiry, pupils will be challenged and supported to:

- Develop contextual knowledge of the location of globally significant places, including their defining physical and human geographical characteristics, and how these provide a geographical context for understanding the actions of geographical processes.

- Understand the processes that give rise to key physical and human features of the world, how these are interdependent and how they bring about spatial variation and change over time.

- Interpret a range of sources of geographical information to reach substantiated conclusions and judgements consistent with the evidence and communicate these in a variety of ways, including through maps, numerical and quantitative skills, and writing at length.

▶Links to Key Stage 3 subject content ◀

Pupils should be taught to:

Locational knowledge

- Extend their locational knowledge and deepen their spatial awareness of the world's countries, including the key physical and human characteristics and major cities of those in Asia.

Human and physical geography

- Understand through the use of detailed place-based exemplars at a variety of scales the key processes in human geography relating to population and urbanisation.

- Understand how human and physical processes interact to influence and change landscapes and environments.

Geographical skills and fieldwork

- Build on their knowledge of globes, maps and atlases and apply and develop this knowledge routinely in the classroom.

- Interpret topographical and thematic mapping, and aerial and satellite photographs.

- Use Geographical Information Systems (GIS) to view, analyse and interpret places and data.

▶Possible assessable outcomes ◀

- A piece of extended explanatory writing which accurately identifies, describes and explains the inter-relationship between the physical environment and human patterns and processes in Japan, including a conclusion consistent with the evidence analysed.

- A presentation which identifies, describes and explains the potential costs and benefits of the three options for increasing airport capacity in Southeast England, including a conclusion in which the pupil presents their considered evaluation of the best option, consistent with the evidence.

Utsobo Tennis Club has 18 public courts including 5 floodlit courts, plus sauna baths, a restaurant and a conference centre.

The land occupied by Utsobo Tennis Club was very expensive – about US$950 per m^2.

Because the land was so expensive to buy, the Utsobo Tennis Club has to charge high prices to people who want to use it, in order to recoup its investment.

Because land prices are high, all available houses and apartments in Osaka are expensive to rent or buy.

Undeveloped areas of land, parks and open spaces without buildings are rare in Osaka.

The lack of space in Osaka means that motorway-like roads called 'expressways' have been built above smaller roads, railways, canals and even buildings.

Because every available plot of land in Osaka has to be used, many houses are built next to noisy railways, expressways and factories.

Yuna earns a salary of US$39,000 a year, but has to work 50 hours a week sometimes and pay rent of US$10,000 a year out of this.

In parts of Osaka, property prices are so high that people have an average of only 4 m^2 of floor space each at home (compared with 36 m^2 in the UK).

Osaka is the third-largest city in Japan (after Tokyo and Yokohama) and is part of the Keihanshin metropolis of Kyoto, Osaka and Kobe, which has a combined population of 19 million.

Yuna has loved playing tennis since she was a pupil at school. She finds it helps her to relax and keep fit.

Yuna lives in the suburbs of Osaka and commutes to her work as a software engineer in the city centre every day.

Despite her salary, Yuna cannot afford to buy a flat of her own and has to share one condominium with two friends who help to cover the rent together.

Because flat and low land in Japan is so scarce, people tend to crowd into the available space, which means that over half the people in the country live on just 5% of its land area.

Because flat land is so scarce, there is only around 20,000 km^2 of building land, or 4.8% of the total available land area in Japan.

Six of Japan's eight largest cities are found in the Tokaido megalopolis, which stretches all the way from Tokyo to Kobe.

About 75% of the land area of Japan is made up of mountains.

Most flat land in Japan occurs in narrow coastal plains which border the sea.

With a small land area and around 130 million people, Japan is the thirteenth most densely populated country in the world.

The Utsobo Tennis Club in Osaka opened in 1996.

Members of the public like Yuna, who live in Osaka, can play tennis 24 hours a day, 365 days a year at the Utsobo Tennis Club.

Osaka is sometimes referred to as the 'nation's kitchen' as it was once the centre of the rice trade, but today it is better known for electronics companies such as Panasonic, Sharp and Sanyo.

Despite working long hours, Yuna tries to play tennis at least twice a week and often at night.

Yuna first started playing tennis at the Utsobo Tennis Club in 2007.

Because space is so limited in Osaka, land prices are very high.

In some parts of the Tokaido megalopolis, population density, a measure of how crowded an area is, reaches 1000 people per km^2. In some Tokyo wards, this figure is as high as 5748 people per km^2 (17% above the national average).

A megalopolis is the name given to a vast and continuous area of towns and cities where conurbations and metropolitan areas have merged into each other.

Yuna Miyakawa is 27 years old and works as a software engineer in Osaka.

Suitable flat land on which to build homes, factories, shops, roads and railways is in short supply all over Japan.

The majority of housing in Osaka is modern, built of concrete, aluminium and wood, but there are also some traditional wooden houses.

Large shopping centres and car parks in Osaka have been built below ground because space is scarce.	The most sparsely populated area of Japan is the northern island of Hokkaido.
Yuna's parents live in Yokohama city and she enjoys visiting them at least once a month. She travels by Shinkansen and the journey takes around three hours.	The largest area of flat land in Japan is along the Pacific coast between the cities of Tokyo and Kobe. This is also the most heavily built and densely populated part of the country.
Japan's rail network is fast, clean and reliable. Osaka also has its own underground network. Yuna's commute takes just over an hour each way.	On average, there are 340 people for each square kilometre of land in Japan, which compares with 257 in the United Kingdom.
Farmland in Japan is always intensively cultivated in order to maximise production from small plots of land.	In many neighbourhoods of Tokyo, rubbish is collected four times a week because residents have nowhere to store it.
It is not unusual in Japan for whole mountains to be levelled in order to create flat land on which to build housing.	In 2013, three of the world's top ten most expensive cities to live in were in Japan.

- When you are writing to explain, your aim is to give clear reasons for a phenomenon, problem, situation or issue.

- The title may be a question, e.g. *How are sedimentary rocks formed? What is global warming?*

- The issue is raised at the start and often summed up at the end.

Text level features often include:

- Diagrams, maps, charts, etc. to provide statistics or illustrate processes.

- An introductory paragraph to provide background information and state the issue or problem.

- A topic sentence at the start of each subsequent paragraph, which makes it clear what the paragraph is about. Paragraphs are used to introduce different reasons or show different stages in a process.

- Headings, subheadings and bullet points might be used to organise the explanation into clear sections.

Sentence level features often include:

- Use of the third person (he, she, it, they) and sometimes the first and second person, to involve the reader, e.g. 'how can we be sure that…', 'you may not think that…'

- Use of the present tense unless referring to a finished action in the past, e.g. 'global warming refers to…', 'the term was first used…'

- Mostly use of active voice, e.g. 'scientists believe that…' However, passive voice can be used to make the text sound more formal or when it is not important to know who did what, e.g. 'it is widely believed that…', 'proposals have been made to…'

- Connectives, which can show: time sequence, e.g. 'in the first place', 'over time', 'eventually'; cause and effect, e.g. 'consequently', 'as a result', 'because'; additional information, e.g. 'also', 'moreover', 'another reason'; and comparison, e.g. 'alternatively', 'whereas', 'but'

Word level features often include:

- Use of specialised and precise vocabulary, e.g. *sediments, compression, particles.*

- Impersonal, factual, plain writing to ensure that the explanation is clear and concise.

What were the causes and effects of the Armenian earthquake of 7 December 1988?

Title often asks a question or states clearly what the explanation is about

Purpose – to explain how and why something happens

Armenia is a small landlocked country about the size of Wales, which can be found to the east of Turkey in Southwest Asia. With a population of three million people it achieved its independence from the Soviet Union in 1988, just a few months before an earthquake devastated much of the stark rocky countryside of the northwest of the country.

Introductory paragraph sets the scene

Present tense throughout

Armenia's geographical location <u>makes it</u> very vulnerable to earthquakes. The country sits on top of the boundary between the Eurasian and Turkish tectonic plates, which rose by 1.5 metres on 7 December 1988. In fact, the boundary is a <u>subduction zone</u>, which means that the Turkish plate is being forced under the Eurasian plate. The resulting shockwaves measured 7.1 on the Richter Scale and were felt throughout the country. The greatest devastation was in the city of Leninakan, which was closest to the earthquake's epicentre.

Technical vocabulary

Topic sentence introduces what the paragraph will be about

Although physical reasons explain why the earthquake happened, <u>many human factors were responsible for making its impact much worse than it should have been.</u> The most important of these was the fact that Armenia lacked the financial resources to incorporate earthquake-proof foundations into the design of new buildings. To house its growing population as cheaply as possible, hundreds of apartment blocks were built with cheap concrete panels, made of cement that contained too much sand.

Connectives show cause and effect

<u>Because</u> the government could not afford to buy heavy plant excavators, most of the apartments were built upon foundations, which were too shallow to support the weight of the building above. Finally, the lack of trained rescue services meant that after the earthquake there was little chance of survivors being located in the rubble or resisting the freezing winter temperatures for long.

Over 60,000 people died on the night of 7 December 1988 and during the weeks that followed the earthquake. The most devastating effects were in Leninakan, where all of the city's 120 apartment blocks collapsed, claiming the lives of one in four of the population. Thousands of others died under buildings in more rural areas, which were cut off completely from outside help for many weeks. As time passed, diseases such as dysentery and diarrhoea took the lives of those who were left with no option but to drink contaminated water. Even today, over half a million Armenians remain homeless, living in tents or portacabins, with little prospect of ever having a permanent home again.

Paragraphs consisting of sentences written in a series of logical steps, usually in time order

Concluding paragraph summarises the key points

The main cause of the 1988 Armenian earthquake was the fact that the country sits astride a major plate boundary, which moves violently from time to time. Natural events such as these are impossible to prevent or predict with the present level of technology. However, many other human factors caused by Armenia's poverty and lack of economic development were also responsible for much of the devastation that occurred on 7 December 1988.

Peer Assessment Sheet: Why can't Yuna play the sport she loves?

	Are these conventions included?	Yes	No	If yes, draw a numbered arrow to show an example in the text	Choose one of the conventions which is missing, or you feel could be improved. Write down your ideas below on how and where in the text it might be included or improved.
1	The introductory paragraph sets the scene and provides background information			Arrow 1	
2	Each paragraph begins with a topic sentence which introduces what it is going to focus on			Arrow 2	
3	Maps, diagrams and photographs are used selectively and provide additional information to that which is written in the text			Arrow 3	
4	Headings, subheadings and bullet points are used to divide the text into clear sections to assist the reader			Arrow 4	
5	Written in the third person			Arrow 5	
6	Written in the present tense			Arrow 6	
7	Use of **active voice**, e.g. 'Geographers believe that...'			Arrow 7	
8	Effective use of connectives to show cause and effect			Arrow 8	
9	Use of appropriate and specialised subject vocabulary			Arrow 9	
10	Plain and impersonal writing to ensure that the explanation is clear and concise			Arrow 10	
11	In the final paragraph, the issue is summarised clearly and a conclusion reached			Arrow 11	

A lack of living space in urban Japan

Flats and apartments

One way of overcoming the problem of space in Japan is, of course, to build upwards. Many families live in high-rise apartment blocks like those shown in the photographs. They can be very small but most will contain at least one bedroom, a small kitchen and living area and a bathroom. Many will also have a balcony. Family homes are generally more spacious than an apartment and are nearly always detached. However, they are very often built very close together with only small gaps between them. Gardens are likely to be small, if indeed there is one. Domestic appliances such as washing machines, tumble-dryers, freezers and boilers are often located outside the home and on balconies because there is insufficient space inside.

Multi-layered parking

Residential areas often have multi-layered car-parking facilities as a means of saving space. This allows for double the storage. The same also applies for bikes. To help maximise the number of bikes that can be stored in any one location, Japan often uses multi-layered bike racks. These types of bike sheds are common near train stations, especially as many people cycle there before catching the train to work and school, etc. There is occasionally a small fee for using the storage system, but bikes will be well looked after. You could ask pupils how they think bikes are elevated to the top layer.

High-rise buildings

Skyscrapers are perhaps the most obvious way of overcoming the problems of congestion. Most cities in Japan will have high-rise buildings in the city centre and they are frequently torn down and replaced with modern, even more efficient equivalents. All new skyscrapers are built to strict guidelines and have to incorporate earthquake-proof measures. As technology advances, the height of the buildings keeps increasing and the shape of buildings becomes ever more inventive.

Transport systems

As a way of saving space regarding transport, many cities now boast multi-layered infrastructure networks. Sometimes, the train lines also run through buildings and go underground as well. 'Bullet' train tracks run separately to regular train tracks. This helps ensure the smooth running of the bullet trains and that they are never slowed down by the regular local trains. Japan also has an extensive underground network to help people travel around.

Roof space

Every spare inch of land is used in Japanese cities and roofs are commonly used for all-weather sports pitches. Most department stores in Japan will have either a rooftop garden, or an outdoor recreational facility, whether it be a restaurant or a sports pitch.

Underground shopping centres

A clever method of saving space has been to develop a network of underground shopping centres in Japan. Nagoya has a particularly large and impressive network of underground shops, ranging from supermarkets to clothes shops.

Tunnels

As Japan is so mountainous, many tunnels have had to be cut through the sides of mountains to make way for the ever-increasing desire for better infrastructure networks. In times gone by, crossing from the Pacific side of Japan to the Japan Sea side was a timely process, with few practical options available other than sea. The mountains made it near impossible for roads to be constructed. By creating a network of tunnels, both major roads and rail lines now connect towns and cities on both sides of the country.

Rush hour

Rush hour in Japan, like any other country, is a busy time on the roads, trains and underground. Shinjuku Station in central Tokyo sees at least two million commuters pass through one of the sixty exits each day. It's a confusing place and very easy to become lost! During peak hours, guards are employed to help push people onto the trains and underground carriages to help keep the traffic moving.

Urban sprawl

Building work takes place on any available flat land in Japan. It only stops when the land becomes too mountainous or gives way to the sea. Around 70% of Japan's population live on 30% of the available land space, so every spare inch is used.

Why should we be concerned about sinkholes?

▶Purpose◀

This investigation is designed to enable pupils to explore how sinkholes affect human activity and whether or not we should be concerned about them. The enquiry begins by telling the story of a teenager who lives in the UK who had her car swallowed by a sinkhole; the idea being that the pupils can empathise with her situation because it could have been them! This is then contrasted with a dramatic sinkhole which opened up in Guatemala City killing several people, highlighting that this is a phenomenon which can potentially occur all over the world.

Pupils are then given a series of images which they use to work out how sinkholes are formed and this is then explained in the text. The geology map of the UK shows High Wycombe's geology to be chalk, which possibly explains the formation of the sinkhole in this location. However, underlying bedrock is not always to blame as sinkholes can appear in the landscape as a result of human activity; broken water pipes and disused mines being the main culprits.

The enquiry then turns towards looking at patterns of geology to determine where sinkholes are most likely to occur. In this section, the USA, and specifically the state of Florida, is the main focus. The combination of Florida's climate, geology and the way in which its citizens use the land lead to the state being called the 'sinkhole capital' of the USA. A resource in the Teacher Book asks pupils to interpret a climate graph for Miami, Florida, and to use this information to work out which month is most likely to coincide with the formation of sinkholes.

Pupils are then asked to consider the effects of sinkholes, which are predominantly negative and can have wide-reaching consequences. However, the positive aspects of sinkholes are then presented, with sinkholes off the coast of Belize drawing in nearly one million tourists each year, all of whom contribute to the local economy and therefore the development of the country. Next, pupils are led through an assessment in which they create a landscape in a shoe-box. Whilst it is important that pupils are allowed to be creative in this task, the quality of the geography should be paramount, so the shoe-box should include clear annotations which describe and explain the location, formation and effects of the sinkhole.

It is also important that pupils draw together their information to answer the key enquiry question, '*Why should we be concerned about sinkholes?*' To that end, a resource in the Teacher Book has examples of annotations which pupils can look at and discuss. The annotations are not meant to be model examples, although some are more precise and detailed than others.

Finally, the enquiry can be extended by pupils considering whether sinkholes are becoming more common by looking at potential future climate patterns and the likely impact of these.

▶ Aims ◀

Through this enquiry, pupils will be challenged and supported to:

- Develop contextual knowledge of the location of globally significant places, including their defining physical and human geographical characteristics, and how these provide a geographical context for understanding the actions of geographical processes.

- Understand the processes that give rise to key physical and human features of the world, how these are interdependent and how they bring about spatial variation and change over time.

- Interpret a range of sources of geographical information to reach substantiated conclusions and judgements consistent with the evidence, and communicate these in a variety of ways, including through maps, numerical and quantitative skills and writing at length.

▶ Links to Key Stage 3 subject content ◀

Pupils should be taught to:

Human and physical geography

Understand, through the use of detailed place-based exemplars at a variety of scales, the key processes in Physical geography relating to: rocks; weathering and soils; weather and climate; and hydrology.

- Understand how human and physical processes interact to influence and change landscapes, environments and the climate, and how human activity relies on the effective functioning of natural systems.

Geographical skills and fieldwork

- Build on their knowledge of globes, maps and atlases, and apply and develop this knowledge routinely in the classroom.

- Interpret topographical and thematic mapping, and aerial and satellite photographs.

▶ Possible assessable outcomes ◀

- A creative piece where the pupils make a sinkhole landscape in a shoe-box. The shoe-box should be annotated with the location, formation and effects of the sinkhole.

Watch the video at http://www.bbc.co.uk/news/science-environment-25983415 which explains the process of solution and how it has the potential to create sinkholes. Now, draw images or diagrams in the boxes to show how this process works. Explain each image with a caption below each box.

Use the climate graph for Miami, Florida, on the right to complete the following sentences:

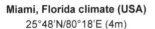

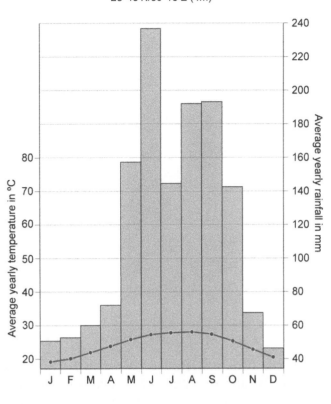

- The highest temperature is _____ °C which occurs in

  the month of _____.

- The lowest temperature is _____ °C which occurs

  in the month of _____.

- The highest precipitation is _____ mm which occurs

  in the month of _____.

- The lowest precipitation is _____ mm which occurs

  in the month of _____.

- The total annual amount of precipitation in

  Miami is _____ mm.

- If I was going to visit Miami in June, the five things that I would pack in my suitcase would be…

  1. _____

  _____

  2. _____

  _____

  3. _____

  _____

  4. _____

  _____

  5. _____

  _____

  Try to explain why you have included each item.

- I would expect most sinkholes to appear in Miami during the month of _____ because…

_____

Belize is a small country with only 300,000 inhabitants, which borders Mexico and Guatemala in the north of Central America. Its strong British colonial heritage makes it culturally very different to the other countries which make up Central America and it is said to have a distinctly 'Caribbean' flavour.

Belize is a country of contrasts in terms of development. It has a Human Development Index (HDI) of 0.732 (2013 figures), which is classified as 'high human development', and is similar to countries like Ukraine, Peru and Macedonia. However, it is also considered to be one of the ten least developed countries in Latin America, with over a third of the population living below the poverty line on less than US$2 per day. There is also a great income disparity, with the poorest 20% of the population living on only 3% of the wealth.

Belize's education system is based on the British one, with pupils spending, on average, twelve years in school. The literacy rate is 70%, although there is a great difference between those who live in urban areas and those who live in remote rural areas, who lack access to schooling and usually drop out of formal education by the age of 12.

Belize's life expectancy is 77 although the population is fairly youthful; only 4% of the population are over 65 whilst 35% are under 14. Belize is also a very happy place to live. According to the 'Happy Planet Index' which combines three indicators – life expectancy, well-being and ecological footprint – Belize is the fourth happiest country in the world, behind Costa Rica, Vietnam and Columbia.

Belize's economy is based upon agriculture, tourism and services, although the recent discovery of crude oil near the town of Spanish Lookout has potential for exploitation. It is challenging for Belize to achieve economic stability due to their reliance upon the export of primary products, particularly citrus, sugar and bananas, which have seen low prices in recent years. There is limited domestic (home) industry due to the small population and the fact that labour costs are relatively high. The tourism industry therefore attracts the most foreign investment, with nearly one million visitors per year. In 2007, the tourist industry was responsible for 25% of jobs in Belize and contributed 18% to GDP, an estimated US$295 million.

Prior to independence (which Belize achieved in 1981), the country was not really suitable for large-scale tourism due to the lack of infrastructure. However, during the last decade there has been massive investment in tourism, which has resulted in positive effects for other industries, including agriculture, commerce, finance and construction. Belize now offers a diverse range of adventure and eco-tourism attractions including the Belize Barrier Reef, offshore islands, caves and Mayan ruins.

- Look at the information in the text and create an infographic which shows Belize's level of development.

- What might be the advantages and disadvantages of Belize developing its tourist industry? Complete the table on the next page – try to think of at least five different things to put into each column.

Advantages of Belize developing its tourism industry	Disadvantages of Belize developing its tourism industry
• Creates jobs (25% of the total for the country) which are more stable than those in agriculture.	• Money generated from tourism may not be reinvested in Belize but may end up abroad in more developed countries.
•	•
•	•
•	•
•	•
•	•
•	•

• On balance, do you think that the tourism industry is a positive thing for Belize or not?

• Imagine that you are planning a holiday to Belize. Which sites would you want to visit? Annotate the blank map below to show your route, what you will visit and why you want to visit each place.

Have a look at the following effects of sinkholes. There are six shown here but you can add your own on the next page. As geographers, we can classify effects into different categories:

- Positive / Negative

- Short-term / Long-term

- Global / National / Local

- Social / Political / Environmental / Economic

Choose one of the ways of classifying effects listed above and colour code the effects below to show the different categories. You may like to choose a second way of classifying if you have the time. How can you use these classifications to make your writing more effective and geographical?

Sinkholes can be tourist attractions and can generate vast amounts of money for the economy.

Sinkholes can cause massive damage to property, which has a knock-on effect increasing the price of house insurance.

Sinkholes can change the general topography of the land and divert streams of underground water.

Sinkholes can cause injury and even death, although this is a fairly rare occurrence.

People living in areas which are susceptible to sinkhole formation can suffer stress and anxiety, even if a sinkhole does not form.

If the land in Florida is not irrigated then crops, such as oranges and strawberries, will not have such high yields. The price of such goods is likely to rise.

Sinkhole in a shoe-box annotations

Below are some annotations which have been used to describe and explain location and formation of the sinkhole in a shoe-box. Read the annotations. What good features do they have? Are there aspects that could be improved? Of the two, which do you think is the best?

Pupil A – location

My sinkhole opened up in Guatemala City in 2010, although this was not the first time a sinkhole had devastated the city. Guatemala City is the capital city of Guatemala which is in Central America. It is next to Mexico, Belize, Honduras and El Salvador. Guatemala also has a coast with the Pacific Ocean.

Pupil A – formation

Sinkholes are usually formed in areas of limestone or chalk. The rock is soluble which means it dissolves when it comes into contact with rainwater. This means that the rock slowly dissolves and leaves large holes underground. Eventually, when the hole is large enough the surface soil cover can collapse taking buildings and people with it!

Pupil B – location

My sinkhole is located in Zone 2 of Guatemala City, the capital city of the Central American country of Guatemala. Guatemala City has a population of over two million and is located in the mountains – it has an altitude of 1500 m. Guatemala itself is a small country bordered by Mexico to the north and west and Belize, Honduras and El Salvador to the east.

Pupil B – formation

Sinkholes can have both physical and human causes. In the case of the sinkhole in Guatemala City, the geology and climate weren't particularly important. The sinkhole was probably caused by broken water pipes under the city streets which overflowed. The rock underneath Zone 2 is volcanic deposits which probably got washed away leaving the streets above unsupported.

2014 saw an increased number of sinkholes affecting the UK compared to previous years. The Met Office claimed that this was likely to be due to the most extreme and intense winter rainfall that England and Wales had seen for nearly 250 years.

- On the map below, and using the website http://www.bgs.ac.uk/research/engineeringGeology/shallowGeohazardsAndRisks/sinkholes/Feb2014.html mark and label the locations of the sinkholes found in 2014 in the UK. Purple icons are sinkholes which are naturally occurring whilst green icons are those caused by human activity.

- Describe the distribution of sinkhole activity.

- Can you explain this distribution? Use the map showing the geology of Great Britain on page 25 of the Student Book to help you.

Do you think that the UK should be prepared for more sinkholes to occur in the future? Why do you think this? How might people living in sinkhole-prone areas in the UK be better prepared?

It has been suggested that sinkholes in Rippon could have inspired Lewis Carroll's *Alice in Wonderland*. Read the story at: http://www.bgs.ac.uk/research/engineeringGeology/shallowGeohazardsAndRisks/Alice_in_wonderland.html

Is fracking all that it's cracked up to be?

Is fracking a sustainable solution to the UK's energy security challenge?

▶**Purpose**◀

The purpose of this enquiry is to investigate the issues surrounding energy security and the sustainability of current approaches to securing energy supplies in the United Kingdom. Whilst developing a detailed knowledge and understanding of the issues surrounding fracking for gas and oil is central to the enquiry, the pupils are also given opportunities to consider a range of alternatives to reliance on fossil fuels – conventional or unconventional – through the use of a geographical decision-making exercise. The enquiry has a UK focus but the approach taken in this enquiry could easily be applied to different countries and contexts, as all nations currently have an energy mix, which will need to change over time.

The enquiry begins by examining the population boom in Williston, North Dakota, USA. The pupils are initially asked to examine the short-term change in land use identifiable in two aerial images from 2009 and 2013, taken from Google Earth. This farmland is outside of Williston, which is at the centre of a remarkable shift in the USA's energy supply. Once the changes have been described, the pupils are challenged to examine the evidence in order to 'tell the story' and suggest reasons for the extraordinary increase in population. Printed copies of the images are a useful way of allowing the pupils to sort the evidence. Williston is located in the middle of the Bakken Formation, a vast shale 'play' that extends across the Canadian border, and fracking of the rocks here is releasing the locked-in hydrocarbons. The discovery and subsequent exploitation of this 'unconventional' energy source has meant that the USA is now no longer reliant on foreign oil imports. The images will allow the pupils to build up their understanding of the energy boom that is driving the population increase, with some real associated challenges for the town of Williston.

The shale gas and oil boom in the USA sets the scene for the rest of this enquiry. In Question 3.2, the pupils are asked to consider and then classify all of the different energy sources in the UK 'energy landscape'. They are also introduced to the underpinning concepts of renewable and non-renewable energy resources and to the term 'energy security'. The UK faces real short- and long-term energy security challenges as fossil fuel reserves from the North Sea decline, at the same time as older nuclear power stations have to be decommissioned and more of the older polluting coal- and gas-fired power stations are closed as a contribution to meeting the UK's carbon emission reduction targets. This combination of factors means that the UK is now a net importer of fossil fuels and needs to invest in new methods of generating electricity in order to meet any future 'energy gap'.

The recent shale energy boom in the USA has had British geologists reconsidering the importance of the abundant shale rocks under many parts of the UK and the government is encouraging the development of a fracking industry to investigate the viability of these reserves. In Question 3.4, the pupils investigate the fracking of shale and the implications this might have for the sustainability of the UK energy mix. The pupils are asked to undertake their own research and to use the resources provided in the Student Book to complete their own fracking enquiry using a suggested 'route to enquiry'. This is a complex and controversial issue so expect a full range of responses. It is important to encourage the pupils to come to a conclusion based on their research. Some time spent discussing the concept of sustainability would be valuable and would also allow the students to delve deeper into the subject and to consider the issue from different perspectives.

Having produced a completed enquiry on fracking in the UK, pupils are led into a final question on possible alternative energy sources to fracking that could contribute to the UK energy mix. It is important that the pupils are given time to explore the details and range of advantages and disadvantages of each energy source discussed. These are provided in the Teacher Book and are intended to provide background information to assist in the Decision-Making Exercise (DME). The DME asks pupils to consider a wide range of energy options for an area of South Devon, with costed proposals attached to the map. The pupils are guided through the decision-making process with further instructions from the Teacher Book. They are encouraged to try to balance costs and benefits, drawing on all elements of this enquiry, in order to reach valid and justifiable conclusions that are supported by sound geographical reasoning and an understanding of a range of energy sources, the concept of an energy mix and the need for sustainable solutions.

▶Aims ◀

Through this enquiry, pupils will be challenged and supported to:

- Develop knowledge and understanding of the concept of sustainability in relation to energy supplies and security by examining the current and projected situation in the UK.

- Explore a contemporary issue from a geographical perspective.

- Understand the physical processes that give rise to energy sources, how the availability of these impacts humans, and how they bring about spatial variation and change over time.

- Interpret a range of sources of geographical information about physical and human processes to reach justifiable geographical decisions with substantiated conclusions and judgements consistent with the evidence. Pupils will learn to communicate these in a variety of ways including through maps, numerical and quantitative skills and writing at length.

- Reflect on their own worldview of current geographical issues and challenges and communicate their feelings and ideas appropriately.

▶Links to Key Stage 3 subject content ◀

Pupils should be taught to:

Locational knowledge

- Extend their locational knowledge and deepen their spatial awareness of the world's countries including the key physical and human characteristics.

Place knowledge

- Understand geographical similarities, differences and links between places.

Human and physical geography

- Understand through the use of detailed place-based exemplars at a variety of scales the key processes in:

  ○ Physical geography relating to geological timescales, rocks weathering and soils.

  ○ Human geography relating to economic activity and the use of natural resources.

- Understand how human and physical processes interact to influence and change landscapes and environments.

Geographical skills and fieldwork

- Build on their knowledge of globes, maps and atlases and apply and develop this knowledge routinely in the classroom.

- Interpret Ordnance Survey maps in the classroom and the field, including using grid references and scale, topographical and other thematic mapping, and aerial and satellite photographs.

- Use Geographical Information Systems (GIS) to view, analyse and interpret places and data.

▶Possible assessable outcomes ◀

- A piece of work that follows a route to geographical enquiry which shows understanding of the issue of fracking in the UK and reaches a reasoned judgement on the role that fracking should play in the future energy mix of the UK, and whether this is a sustainable approach. There are other assessment opportunities in the DME, which could be used to assess knowledge and understanding of a range of energy sources, and the role they could play in meeting the energy needs of small areas, as well as the pupils' ability to make and communicate geographical decisions.

Are our energy sources renewable or non-renewable?

Energy source	Advantages include:	Disadvantages include:
Coal: fossil fuel	• Cheap and plentiful supplies	• Highly polluting • Will eventually run out
Shale oil and gas: fossil fuel	• Shale rocks are very common • Cheaper to extract than oil and gas in deep water	• The shale needs to be fractured by lots of wells • A fossil fuel that contributes to carbon emissions
Onshore wind	• 'Clean' energy source • Wind can be used again and again	• Local opposition can stop planning permission being granted • Wind isn't always reliable
Oil: fossil fuel	• One barrel of oil produces a huge amount of energy	• Difficult to drill and transport safely • Highly polluting • Is running out
Nuclear	• Highly efficient • Can produce huge amounts of electricity from relatively little uranium	• Very expensive to build and run • Risk from nuclear accidents • Nuclear waste will be radioactive for thousands of years
Hydro electric power (HEP)	• 'Clean' energy source • HEP dams have other uses, e.g. domestic water supply • Uses the continuous movement of water in the hydrological cycle	• Can damage downstream ecosystems • Dams are expensive to build

Energy source table

Energy source	Advantages include:	Disadvantages include:
Biomass	• Uses plants/trees which can be regrown quickly and locally	• Adds to greenhouse gas emissions
Tidal power	• Tidal stream generators have little ecosystem impact • The tide is reliable and predictable	• Challenging to build and maintain
Wave energy	• 'Clean' and plentiful energy source	• Complicated to build
Solar power	• 'Clean' energy source • The sun is a very reliable energy source	• Expensive to build
Natural gas: fossil fuel	• Cleaner than coal and oil	• Burning emits CO_2 • Will run out
Geothermal	• 'Clean' energy source • Heat source is reliable	• Can only be built in certain tectonically active places
Offshore wind	• Can take advantage of more reliable wind speed • Away from population centres	• Harder to build and maintain

Name	Nuclear power
Key information	Generating electricity in a nuclear power station uses uranium or plutonium to create controlled nuclear fission reactions. These generate heat, which is used to create steam, which is used to turn giant turbines. These spin and generate electricity. The UK has plans to build seven new nuclear plants by 2030.
Example location	Hinkley Point A, B and C (under construction)
Benefits	• Nuclear power doesn't depend on fossil fuels • CO_2 emissions are limited • Will help guarantee energy supplies • The UK can close older coal-fired power stations • They provide jobs for people in their design, construction and operation • Local economies benefit from the investment • Each new reactor will generate up to 1.6 gigawatts – enough to power a city the size of Manchester – and should last for sixty years
Costs	• Most of the UK's CO_2 emissions come from transport and industry so nuclear power won't have a huge effect on this • Every pound spent on nuclear is a pound less spent on renewable technology • Uranium and plutonium are finite resources, so will run out eventually • Mining, refining and transporting uranium and plutonium causes environmental impacts • There is no current satisfactory long-term solution to where we put toxic radioactive waste, which lasts for thousands of years • A by-product of power generation is material used to create nuclear weapons • A nuclear accident (like at Chernobyl or Fukushima) could be devastating for the UK • They are built at coastal locations, possibly vulnerable to sea level rise

Name	Wind energy
Key information	The UK is the windiest country in Europe. One modern 2.5 megawatt turbine is capable of generating enough electricity to power 1400 homes. Groups of turbines are called wind farms and these can be located either on or offshore. The UK currently has 632 separate wind projects containing 5492 turbines. Combined, these generate over 11,000 megawatts of power – enough to power 6.2 million homes. These wind farms reduce the UK carbon footprint by over eleven million tonnes per year.
Example location	The Thannet offshore wind farm in Kent
Benefits	• Uses clean, renewable energy source • Cheap to operate once built • Zero emissions so benefits health and UK carbon footprint • Reduces reliance on fossil fuel imports, more energy security in the future
Costs	• No wind = no power • Some people oppose them if they live nearby • Electricity from wind currently costs more per unit than from fossil fuels • The windiest places are more remote (hill tops or offshore) so maintenance can be challenging

Name	Wave and tidal power
Key information	As an island nation, the UK have some of the largest tidal ranges in the world and waves from the west and southwest have often travelled thousands of miles across the Atlantic Ocean. It is possible to generate electricity from the ocean by harnessing the movement of the waves and the incoming and outgoing tide. There are four methods: • Nearshore wave power – harnessing wave energy as they break • Offshore wave power – harnessing wave movement in deeper water • Tidal stream power – turbines harnessing the tide as it moves past • Tidal range power – trapping the high tide behind a barrage and releasing it to generate electricity
Example location	The Islay Limpet, Scotland The Cornish Wave Hub Tidal stream project in Orkney, Scotland Tidal Lagoon, Swansea
Benefits	• All generate clean, renewable electricity and help decarbonise the UK • There are multiple suitable locations around the UK for wave power • The UK is the global leader in developing this technology, so more green jobs will be created • Wave and tidal power will generate over 120 MW by 2020, making a meaningful contribution to the UK's energy mix • Combined wave and tidal power has the potential to provide 20% of the UK's electricity
Costs	• There are high upfront costs involved with tidal power and there are less suitable locations than for wave power • Tidal and wave energy could disrupt marine life • Tidal energy is difficult to transport and is intermittent although predictable • Wave energy can be very intermittent • Offshore wave farms could disrupt marine navigation • Nearshore wave farms have a visual impact on the coast

Name	Geothermal
Key information	Geothermal power harnesses the heat of the earth's crust to generate electricity. This is quite straightforward in some places – Iceland for example, which sits on a constructive plate boundary and a hot spot. Almost everywhere, the upper 3 m of the earth's surface is between 10–16 °C, heated by the sun. This can be harnessed by ground source heat pumps. The further down we go, the hotter it gets, even away from tectonic activity – up to 30 °C per km in areas of granite. This heat can be harnessed to generate electricity by drilling boreholes and pumping high-pressure heated water up to the surface and converting it to steam to drive the generator turbines. These flash steam plants then cool the steam which condenses to water. It is then injected back into the ground to be used again.
Example location	Iceland is the world leader in geothermal energy The UK has a geothermal heat plant in Southampton The Eden Project has plans to build a hot rock system in Cornwall
Benefits	• A renewable energy source that reduces reliance on fossil fuels and energy imports • It is low carbon, so helps to reduce CO_2 emission from electricity generation • Very low running costs, so cheaper electricity
Costs	• Drilling operations can be disruptive • Limited large scale potential in the UK, not everywhere is suitable • High installation costs • Drilling and operations may release harmful gases

Name	Solar energy
Key information	The earth receives an astonishing amount of energy from the sun. In 1838, physicist Sir John Herschel conducted a simple experiment to calculate how much energy is radiated from the sun. He calculated it radiates enough energy to power ten 100 watt light bulbs for every square meter of the surface. He went further to calculate the total energy radiated from the sun into space: an astonishing 400 million million million million watts. This is the equivalent of a million times the annual power consumption of the USA being radiated every second. Solar energy can be harnessed by: • Photo Voltaic Cells or solar panels • Concentrated solar power using mirrors to focus solar energy at the top of a tower
Example location	Shams CSP Plant, Abu Dhabi Senftenberg Solarpark, Germany
Benefits	• A renewable, clean energy source with no air pollution • Reduces reliance on foreign energy imports • Easy to maintain • Silent in operation and can be small scale
Costs	• The initial setup cost is high • The UK has less solar potential as you move further north • It is intermittent and can be hard to store the energy • Solar energy cannot produce energy as quickly or as cheaply as fossil fuels

Name	Hydro electric power (HEP)
Key information	HEP uses the power of moving water to turn turbines which generate electricity. Schemes can be small or large scale. Humans have used HEP for centuries to run mills. There are two distinct ways of generating HEP from rivers: • Building dams • Building run-of-the-river systems that use the change in height of a river as it moves downstream
Example location	The Three Gorges Dam, China The Hoover Dam, Arizona–Nevada border, USA
Benefits	• A renewable source of energy • No pollution and/or greenhouse gases emitted from electricity generation • A dam is often a multipurpose scheme. It helps flood control, water supplies and irrigation, and creates leisure, recreation and tourism opportunities • Water can be stored and used to generate power when demand is high • HEP schemes are long lasting so can be relied upon for decades
Costs	• Dams are very expensive to build and maintain and will disrupt river ecosystems • Dams flood large areas behind them after completion, causing social impacts • Dams can also cause conflict between countries where rivers cross international borders • Run-of-the-river systems can disrupt river environments and natural processes

In this task you are going to be making decisions about the energy future of an area of Devon in the United Kingdom.

The Department of Energy and Climate Change has asked all local councils to identify ways that they can contribute to increasing the security of the UK energy mix. A team of energy advisors have drawn up a set of proposals for Teignbridge District Council to demonstrate how electricity could be generated in the area. Each option has a range of costs and benefits.

To make a decision as to which proposal or proposals they will recommend to the government, they need you to consider:

- The environmental impact of each proposal, positive and negative.

- How far the schemes will go toward providing electricity for Teignmouth (6365 households), Newton Abbot (9751 households) or the whole of Teignbridge (51,417 households).

- How sustainable each option is. Does it meet the needs of the area now and in the future?

- The total cost of their recommendations.

Tasks:

1 Create a table to identify the advantages and disadvantages of each proposal. How sustainable is each option?

2 Rank each site from 1–10 in terms of cost: 10 most expensive – 1 least expensive.

3 Rank each site from 1–10 in terms of power output: 1 highest – 10 lowest.

4 Divide the cost by the potential power output to calculate the cost per home.

5 Make a decision on which proposals you will recommend to the government.

6 You need to consider the costs, benefits and level of sustainability of each one.

7 Write a report to the government in which you must outline:

- Why there is a need to change the current UK energy mix. Think about local, national and global issues.

- Which proposals you are recommending and why.

- The total cost and power output of your recommendations.

- Which proposals you rejected and why.

- A concluding statement, which summarises the issues briefly and makes clear the decision you are recommending.

Are there alternatives?

Throughout this enquiry you have been investigating a range of issues surrounding our consumption of energy. Finding solutions to these issues is vital to the future energy security of the UK. The UK energy mix currently relies heavily upon using finite fossil fuels to provide us with power in our homes. There are many issues related to this reliance on fossil fuels such as air pollution, climate change and a reliance on energy sources from other nations, so we need a new generation of people to make decisions about our energy future.

The UK has three different approaches for you to consider:

- Business as usual – maintain use of fossil fuels and seek stable and secure supplies from other countries when our supplies are exhausted.

- A multi-energy solution – diversify our energy sources to make best use of what we have in the UK.

- Energy conservation – reduce the amount of energy consumed.

Making decisions on the most sustainable and effective way forward forms the basis of this task. Read the instructions very carefully. They will tell you what to do and they will tell you how your work will be assessed.

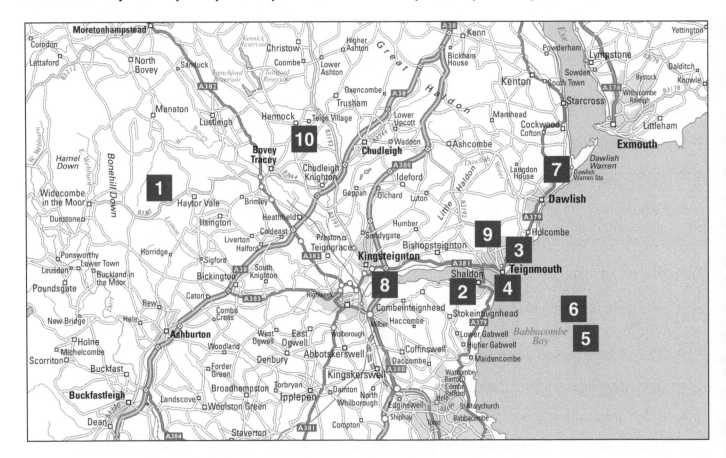

Figure A: *Suggested sites for energy generation in South Devon*

Site	Proposal	Useful information	Cost	Potential power output
1	Onshore wind farm	• Build five 2.5 MW turbines • Very windy location • Inaccessible • In Dartmoor National Park – very strict planning guidelines	US$16 million	Will power 7700 homes
2	Hydro electric plants	• Build one 2 MW river-based power plant using water flow and height change to generate power • No dam required • Variable power output • Could build more than one on River Teign	US$8.3 million	Will power 1800 homes
3	Small onshore wind farm	• Build five 0.1 MW turbines on Teignmouth seafront • Accessible and flat site • Faces east so wind likely to be variable	US$2.9 million	Will power 245 homes
4	Tidal stream generator	• Build seven 1.5 MW Sea Gen tidal stream generators underwater at mouth of River Teign • Need to be small enough to allow shipping to pass at high tide • May impact local fishermen as access to the area will become restricted	US$116 million	Will power 10,000 homes
5	Offshore wave generator	• Twenty-six Pelamis wave generators installed and connected to electricity grid via an undersea cable • Area could no longer be fished	US$132 million	Will power 13,000 homes
6	Offshore wind farm	• Ten 3 MW wind turbines built five miles offshore • Will be visible on a clear day from land • Power comes to shore via undersea cable	US$129 million	Will power 20,000 homes
7	Micro nuclear plant	• Small nuclear reactor buried in concrete under ground at Dawlish Warren • Site is a SSSI (Site of Special Scientific Interest) and a nature reserve • Reactor needs refuelling every 7–10 years • Cost covers installation but not waste processing, which will be very expensive	US$26.5 million	Will power 20,000 homes
8	Biomass power station	• Will burn wood from sustainably managed forests across the southwest • Built on flat land adjoining the race course • Higher CO_2 emissions than other options	US$55 million	Will power 31,000 homes
9	Solar PV panels	• Install solar panels on the roofs of 2000 properties • Households can sell back unused energy to the grid for profit	US$58 million	Will power 2000+ homes
10	Engineered geothermal system	• Develop geothermal power by drilling into the granite on Dartmoor. This could be done outside of the boundaries of the National Park.	US$25 million	Will power 4000 homes
11	Energy conservation scheme	• The council can promote energy conservation through the education of children at local schools, free home insulation programmes, the distribution of energy saving light bulbs and smart meters. They will appoint ten energy advisors to carry out this work locally.	US$3.3 million	Will reduce electricity consumption in each household

Why did the earth nearly die at the end of the Permian period?

▶Purpose◀

This enquiry has been designed to enable pupils to engage with and understand the concept of geologic or deep time. Both the chronology and significance of geologic time are often quite challenging for young people to comprehend, given the enormity of a 4.6 billion year timeline. To help pupils engage with geological time, the investigation begins with defining and exploring the extent of history and prehistory through practical and interactive learning activities based outside the classroom. This enables pupils to comprehend the story of the earth from its origin nearly five billion years ago and to appreciate the infinitesimally tiny proportion of its life that has seen periods of human prehistory and history. Pupils are encouraged to see the evolution of geologic time linked to the constant movements of landmasses around the globe as a story which reveals tantalising glimpses into our past. Throughout the enquiry, pupils are supported to make links with the present and to see how events which happened in deep geologic time, billions of years ago, still influence patterns of human and physical geography across the globe today. Being able to visualise the pattern of movement of the ancient landmass of Pangea, together with understanding the dynamic nature of the present day distribution of continents and oceans and how the earth might look 100 million years from now, is central to the investigation.

The bulk of the enquiry focuses on one period of geologic time, the Permian, and challenges pupils to solve one of the greatest mysteries of deep time; an event that nearly exterminated all life on Earth. The end of the Permian period 252 million years ago was marked by a catastrophic event of some kind, which wiped out 96% of all living things. In its 4.6 billion year history, the earth has never come as close to extinction. Remarkably, 4% of living things survived and formed the gene pool from which human beings evolved. Through investigating the English Riviera Global Geopark, the pupils are able to gain an insight into what the Permian environment of the land that now comprises the United Kingdom was like over 250 million years ago. They are also able to appreciate why UNESCO designates places around the world with important geological stories to tell as Global Geoparks and to find out about one of these in more detail.

The cause of the Great Dying at the end of the Permian period remains to this day one of the greatest mysteries of the earth. Pupils are invited to examine the merits of the main alternative theories: asteroid impact; massive volcanic eruptions; climate change; and methane release associated with a huge drop in oxygen levels in the ocean. Through interacting with a range of resources, the pupils are supported to evaluate and critique the various arguments and to reach independent conclusions consistent with the evidence. Most palaeontologists are agreed that there is little evidence to support an asteroid impact theory and a good deal of convincing evidence that the remaining 'suspects in the greatest murder mystery of all time' all had a hand in bringing about the disaster. Pupils are encouraged to understand and make links between a number of events occurring as a 'chain reaction' 252 million years ago that ultimately probably led to the mass extinction, or Great Dying, on Earth.

Finally, the pupils are challenged to apply their knowledge and skills as they design a piece of children's play equipment to represent the Great Dying, to go in the Permian zone of the English Riviera Geoplay Park at Paignton, and an interpretation panel to go nearby to tell the story for adults and carers who accompany their children to the play park.

▶ Aims ◀

Through this enquiry, pupils will be challenged and supported to:

- Appreciate the extent of geologic timescales compared with prehistoric and historic time, and the manner in which geological events of the past influence present day patterns of human and physical geography.

- Develop contextual knowledge of the location of globally significant places, including their defining physical and human geographical characteristics, and how these provide a geographical context for understanding the actions of geographical processes.

- Understand the processes that give rise to key physical and human features of the world, how these are interdependent and how they bring about spatial variation and change over time.

- Interpret a range of sources of geographical information about physical and human processes to reach substantiated conclusions and judgements consistent with the evidence and interpret and communicate these in a variety of ways, including through models, maps, numerical and quantitative skills and writing at length.

- Reflect on their own worldview of current geographical issues and challenges, and communicate their feelings and ideas appropriately.

▶ Links to Key Stage 3 subject content ◀

Pupils should be taught to:

Locational knowledge

- Extend their locational knowledge and deepen their spatial awareness of the world's countries, including the key physical and human characteristics of Russia.

Place knowledge

- Understand geographical similarities, differences and links between places.

Human and physical geography

- Understand through the use of detailed place-based exemplars at a variety of scales the key processes in physical geography relating to geological timescales and plate tectonics.

- Understand how human and physical processes interact to influence and change landscapes, environments and the climate, and how human activity relies on effective functioning of natural systems.

Geographical skills and fieldwork

- Build on their knowledge of globes, maps and atlases, and apply and develop this knowledge routinely in the classroom and in the field.

- Interpret topographical and thematic mapping, and aerial and satellite photographs.

- Use Geographical Information Systems (GIS) to view, analyse and interpret places and data.

▶ Possible assessable outcomes ◀

- The design and construction of a piece of children's play equipment, which represents the story of the Great Dying or mass extinction, which occurred at the end of the Permian period.

- An interpretation panel for adults at the same play park, which presents in an engaging manner the different theories for the mass extinction, evaluates and critiques the merits of each argument, and presents a personal conclusion consistent with the current evidence.

55 BC Roman General Julius Caesar invades Britain	787 The Vikings begin to raid the northeast sea coast of Britain	1066 William of France defeats King Harold at the Battle of Hastings and is crowned King of England
1192 King Richard I leads the Crusades to the Holy Land	1215 The Magna Carta is signed	1348 The Black Death comes to Britain
1529 Henry VIII makes himself Head of the Church of England	1588 The Spanish Armanda is destroyed by the English Navy	1603 King James I becomes the first king of England *and* Scotland
1605 The Gunpowder Plot to blow up King James I and the Houses of Parliament is planned	1642 The English Civil War begins	1666 The Great Fire of London occurs
1707 The country of Great Britain comes into existence	1815 The wars against Napoleon and France end	1825 The first passenger railway in Britain (and in the world) begins running
1838 Slavery is abolished in Britain and in all her territories	1881 Primary school education is made compulsory for boys and girls	1914 World War I begins

1939 World War II begins	1978 The first personal computer goes on sale	1982 Britain fights a war with Argentina to keep control of the Falkland Islands
1997 Diana, Princess of Wales is killed in a car accident in Paris	2011 The wedding of Prince William and Kate Middleton	2012 London holds the Olympic and Paralympic Games
1974 Britain joins the Common Market of Europe	1968 The first colour television goes on sale	1994 The Channel Tunnel opens
1952 Princess Elizabeth becomes Queen Elizabeth II	1868 The last public execution is carried out in Britain	1775 The American War of Independence begins
1170 Archbishop of Canterbury Thomas Becket is assassinated	1415 A major English victory in France at the Battle of Agincourt occurs	1086 Work on the Domesday Book begins
122 Work begins to construct Hadrian's Wall	60 Boudica of the Iceni leads a revolt against Roman occupation	40 Roman Emperor Caligula plans an invasion of Britain

4.6 billion ybp	4.5 billion ybp	4.4 billion ybp
The earth forms from dust clouds	The earth's core forms as dense metals sink to the centre	Evidence of the oldest known minerals to form on Earth

4 billion ybp	3.7 billion ybp	3.5 billion ybp
Evidence of the earth's oldest known crustal rocks	The earliest signs of photosynthesising bacteria	Evidence of fossils of rock-eating bacteria

2.1 billion ybp	1.5 billion ybp	700 million ybp
Oxygen begins to form in the atmosphere	The first *eukaryotes* appear – the basic cell type that almost every other living thing is made of	Earliest trace fossils of animal life

600 million ybp	500 million ybp	400 million ybp
First multi-celled animals	Animals with skeletons and the earliest fish evolve	Plants evolve from algae and cover the land

300 million ybp	200 million ybp	140 million ybp
The first amphibians leave the oceans	Lizards evolve into dinosaurs	The first bird evolves from feathered dinosaurs

130 million ybp	50–60 million ybp	35 million ybp
Flowering plants appear	Mass extinction of the dinosaurs	The first primates (monkeys) evolve

15 million ybp Grass appears	2.5 million ybp The first species of humans – *Homo habilis* evolves	1.3 million ybp Ice Ages begin
2 million ybp *Homo erectus* is the first species of modern humans to migrate across Europe and Asia	500–700,000 ybp The earliest evidence of modern human beings in Britain	100,000 ybp The last glaciation in Britain comes to an end

The Permian Extinction – When Life Nearly Came to an End

http://science.nationalgeographic.com/prehistoric-world/permian-extinction/

Written by Hillel J. Hoffman
Republished from the pages of *National Geographic* magazine

'Welcome to the Black Triangle,' said paleobiologist Cindy Looy as our van slowed to a stop in the gentle hills of the northern Czech Republic, a few miles from the German and Polish borders. The Black Triangle gets its name from the coal burned by nearby power plants. Decades of acid rain generated by power-plant emissions have devastated the region's ecosystems. For months I'd been on the trail of the greatest natural disaster in Earth's history. About 250 million years ago, at the end of the Permian period, something killed some 90 percent of the planet's species. Less than 5 percent of the animal species in the seas survived. On land less than a third of the large animal species made it. Nearly all the trees died. Looy had told me that the Black Triangle was the best place today to see what the world would have looked like after the Permian extinction.

We saw the first signs of death as we walked into the hills – hundreds of fallen timbers lay hidden in the undergrowth. A forest once grew here. Half a mile (0.8 kilometres) uphill we found the trunks of a stand of spruce, killed by acid rain. No birds called, no insects hummed. The only sound was the wind through the acid-tolerant weeds.

Looy picked up a spruce cone. Pollen from the trees around us might be preserved inside. She believes that the Permian extinction was caused by acid rain following a massive release of volcanic gases. She wants to compare tree pollen from a modern forest killed by acid rain with fossil pollen found in Permian rocks.

Like a homicide detective at a crime scene, Looy sealed the cone in a plastic bag for later lab work. 'You could say we're working on the greatest murder mystery of all time,' she said.

Looy is one of many scientists trying to identify the killer responsible for the largest of the many mass extinctions that have struck the planet. The most famous die-off ended the reign of the dinosaurs 65 million years ago between the Cretaceous and Tertiary periods. Most researchers consider that case closed. Rocks of that age contain traces of an asteroid that struck Earth, generating catastrophic events from global wildfires to climate change. But the Permian detectives are faced with a host of suspects and not enough evidence to convict any of them.

To understand this extinction, I wanted first to get a sense of its scale. That's difficult – sediments containing fossils from the end of the Permian are rare and often inaccessible. One site that preserves the extinction's victims lies about a half day's drive inland from Cape Town, South Africa, in a scrubland known as the Karoo.

'The Karoo is the kind of place where people fall asleep at the wheel,' said Roger Smith, a paleontologist at the South African Museum, as we drove across the treeless land. 'But it may be the best place to see the terrestrial realm's transition from the Permian to the Triassic period.'

We ascended through sheep-ranching country toward the Lootsberg Pass. The rocks that surrounded us date from the late Permian. For every yard of altitude we gained, we travelled tens of thousands of years forward in time, heading for the Permian's conclusion. If we had driven here before the extinction, we would have seen animals as abundant and diverse as those of today's Serengeti, except most would have belonged to a group known as synapsids. Often called

mammal-like reptiles – they looked like a cross between a dog and a lizard – the synapsids were Earth's first great dynasty of land vertebrates.

'We've found fossils of many kinds of synapsids in these rocks, especially tortoise-beaked dicynodonts, which likely lived in herds and browsed on vegetation along the riverbanks,' said Smith. 'There were also a lot of smaller grazers and root grubbers, like *Diictodon*, a dachshund-shaped dicynodont that probably dug up roots and shoots. They were preyed upon by gorgonopsians – fleet-footed synapsid carnivores with needle-sharp teeth.'

The late Permian rocks we passed as we neared Lootsberg Pass capture the synapsids at the height of their reign. For more than 60 million years they were Earth's dominant land vertebrates, occupying the same ecological niches as their successors, the dinosaurs.

Smith slowed at a switchback, rolled down the window, and pointed to a horizontally banded cliff. 'See that road cut?' he asked. 'That's your Permo-Triassic transition zone. Brace yourself, you're about to go through the extinction.' The fossils embedded in this road cut suggest that synapsids took a savage hit at the end of the Permian.

A synapsid known as *Lystrosaurus* appears in these sediments. Smith had a skull of the animal in his truck. Its flat face gave it the look of a bulldog with tusks. In the first few yards of the transition zone, only one or two *Lystrosaurus* fossils have been found scattered among all the diverse late Permian animals. Higher up, the diversity suddenly dwindles. Dozens of species of Permian synapsids disappear, leaving *Lystrosaurus* and a few others in early Triassic rocks. Animals were still abundant, but the community they formed was about as species rich as a cornfield.

Plants were also hit by the extinction. Evidence for the scale of damage to the world's forests comes from the Italian Alps. I joined a research team led by Henk Visscher of the University of Utrecht at the Butterloch gorge, where exposed fossil beds cover the transition from the Permian to the Triassic. The beds lie high on a cliff, accessible only by climbing piles of debris. I anxiously followed veteran climber Mark Sephton up a slope of loose rocks to a ledge. Sephton used his hammer to chip bits of rock from the layers that chronicle the extinction. Each fragment contains microscopic fossils – pieces of plants and fungi. The lower layers, dating from prior to the extinction, contain lots of pollen, typical of a healthy conifer forest. But in rocks from the Permo-Triassic boundary the pollen is replaced by strands of fossilized fungi – as many as a million segments in some golf-ball-size rocks.

All that fungi in boundary rocks may represent an exploding population of scavengers feasting on an epic meal of dead trees. 'We think it's a wood-decaying fungus,' says Looy, who works with Visscher. 'When a tree dies, it falls. As it decays, fungi grow into it from spores on the ground, decomposing it.'

Visscher and his colleagues have found elevated levels of fungal remains in Permo-Triassic rocks from all over the world. They call it a 'fungal spike.' The same rocks yield few tree pollen grains. Visscher's conclusion: Nearly all the world's trees died en masse.

On the drive from Butterloch a team member handed me a soft, brown banana – a leftover from lunch. 'This is how you can imagine the Permian extinction,' he said. 'Rotting biomass.'

'It's not easy to kill so many species,' says Doug Erwin, a Smithsonian Institution paleontologist. 'It had to be something catastrophic.' Erwin and geologist Samuel Bowring of the Massachusetts Institute of Technology have dated volcanic ash in Chinese sediments laid down during the extinction. Bowring thinks the extinction took place in as little as 100,000 years – quicker than the click of a camera shutter on a geologic scale of time. Suspects must be capable of killing with staggering swiftness both on land and in the seas. As I spoke with some of the researchers on the killer's trail, I learned how many suspects there are – and how difficult it is to develop a tight case.

An enormous asteroid impact is the prime suspect of Gregory Retallack, a geologist at the University of Oregon. The collision would have sent billions of particles into the atmosphere, he explains. They would have spread around the planet, then rained down on land and sea.

Retallack has discovered tiny quartz crystals marked with microscopic fractures in rocks from the time of the extinction in Australia and Antarctica. 'You need staggering force, many times greater than a nuclear explosion, to create this shocked quartz,' said Retallack. 'Only an impact could deform it this way.' A team of researchers recently found what may be that impact's footprint buried below Australia – a 75-mile-wide (120-kilometer-wide) crater left by an asteroid more than three miles (4.8 kilometers) across.

I asked Retallack what an impact would be like if we had been standing a few hundred miles from ground zero. 'You'd feel a shudder,' he replied. 'Clouds of noxious gases would billow in and block out the sun for months. Temperatures would drop, and corrosive acid snow and rain would fall. After the clouds cleared, the atmosphere would be thick with carbon dioxide from fires and decaying matter. CO_2 is a greenhouse gas; it would have contributed to global warming that lasted millions of years.'

The short-term effects alone – cold, darkness, and acid rain – would kill plants and photosynthetic plankton, the base of most food chains. Herbivores would starve, as would the carnivores that fed on the plant-eaters.

Other Permian detectives suspect the killer oozed up from the sea. For years scientists have known that the deep ocean lacked oxygen in the late Permian. But most life is concentrated in shallow water, in places like reefs. In 1996 English geologists Paul Wignall and Richard Twitchett of the University of Leeds reported the first evidence of oxygen depletion, or anoxia, in rocks that formed under shallow water at the time of the extinction.

Pollution sometimes turns waters anoxic today in regions that lack good circulation. Local die-offs of marine life can result. But Wignall suspects that the entire ocean may have stagnated in Permian times. What could still the currents that oxygenate the ocean? Perhaps a lack of ice caps during the late Permian led to the stagnation. Normally temperature differences between polar and equatorial waters create convective currents. Without those currents, anoxic water could have built up, spilling into shallow water as sea levels rose and smothering marine life.

Permian oceans also might have been poisoned with CO_2, according to Andrew Knoll, a paleobiologist at Harvard. Oceanic bacteria eat organic matter, producing bicarbonate as a digestive by-product. Without currents, the load of bicarbonate could have grown in the deep ocean. Knoll thinks something big – he's not sure what – disturbed the seas. Bicarbonate-laden water rose from below, he suggests. As it did, it depressurized. Dissolved bicarbonate was released as CO_2, making the seas bubble at times like a glass of soda.

The crisis for marine animals would have started when toxic levels of CO_2 entered the shallows. Fish would have grown lethargic and slowly fallen asleep. 'Perhaps the Permian ended with a whimper and not a bang,' said Knoll.

Another suspect – a deadly epoch of volcanic eruptions – left a million-square-mile (2.6-million-square-kilometer) fingerprint in Siberia. Below the town of Norilsk lies a two-and-a-half-mile-thick (four-kilometer-thick) pile of lava, overgrown by conifers. Geologists call this vast lava field the Siberian Traps. It wasn't produced by one volcano. 'Thick, pulsing flows of glowing magma gushed out from numerous broad, flat volcanoes,' said geologist Paul Renne of the Berkeley Geochronology Center. 'Hundreds of cubic miles spread across Siberia – enough to cover the Earth to a depth of about 20 feet (6 meters).'

For decades scientists have known the Siberian Traps were formed around the time of the Permian extinction. Could the greatest extinction be related to the greatest volcanic eruptions? Renne, an expert at determining the ages of rocks, has been trying to work out the timing of the events. His lab is filled with machines – tangles of high-voltage cables, vacuum lines, and stainless steel – that date rocks by measuring the decay of radioactive isotopes within them. Renne secured chunks of lava from the Siberian Traps and Permo-Triassic boundary rocks from China. He has determined the two events occurred within 100,000 years of each other. Renne doubts that's a coincidence.

But the Siberian Traps volcanoes didn't cause the extinction by swamping the world with lava. As volcanic gases poured into the skies, they would have generated acid rain, and sulfate molecules would have blocked sunlight and cooled the planet. Glaciation would have reduced the volume of water in the ocean, storing it as ice. Sea level would have dropped, killing marine life in the shallows and severely reducing diversity. Lowering sea level can also release the ocean's methane, which, combined with CO_2 from the eruptions and decaying organic matter, would likely produce greenhouse conditions. 'In 1783 a volcano called Laki erupted in Iceland,' said Renne. 'Within a year global temperature dropped almost two degrees. Imagine a Laki erupting every year for hundreds of thousands of years.'

Each scientist I met left me thinking that he or she was a clue or two away from solving the crime. But as Doug Erwin of the Smithsonian cautioned me, 'the truth is sometimes untidy.' The Permian extinction reminds him of Agatha Christie's *Murder on the Orient Express*, in which a corpse with 12 knife wounds is discovered on a train. Twelve different killers conspired to slay the victim. Erwin suspects there may have been multiple killers at the end of the Permian. Maybe everything – eruptions, an impact, anoxia – went wrong at once.

Could it happen again? 'Sure,' Erwin replied. 'The question is when. Tomorrow? A hundred million years from now?'

I left Erwin's office at the Smithsonian and wandered into the dinosaur hall. Behind the dinosaurs was a case with skulls of Permian synapsids. They don't get many visitors. *Lystrosaurus*, the synapsid that inherited the barren world of the Triassic, stared out empty-eyed. With its competition gone, *Lystrosaurus* spread across the world, from Russia to Antarctica.

Death creates opportunity. Survivors occupy vacant niches. Within a million years synapsid diversity recovered. One lineage produced our ancestors, the first mammals. Now we are creating a new mass extinction, wiping out countless species. Will life be as resilient this time? I remembered the acid-tolerant plants of the Black Triangle, where we've done so much to destroy an ecosystem. If life can survive the Permian extinction, it can survive anything.

Although methane levels in the atmosphere at the time of the Great Dying were hundreds of times the levels experienced today, geographers are still concerned about methane. This is because methane is one of the most potent greenhouse gases with the ability to trap twenty-nine times more heat per mass unit than carbon dioxide. Have a look at the graphs of Major Greenhouse Gas Trends 1975–2015 below, then answer the following questions:

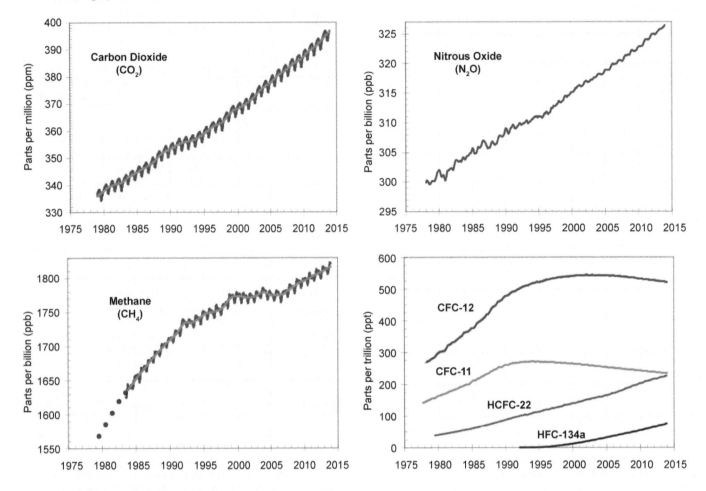

1 How does the trend line for the build-up of methane in the atmosphere compare with the trend lines for carbon dioxide and nitrous oxide?

2 What do you think may have caused a levelling off in the rate of methane build-up between 1988 and 2007?

3 What are the main sources of methane release into the atmosphere today?

4 Which of these do you think can be classified as **natural** and which are **anthropogenic** (human caused)?

5 What are the CFC, HCFC and HFC greenhouse gases shown in the graphs and what are their main sources?

Sequence of events leading up to the Great Dying at the end of the Permian period

Name of event	Description of event (what occurred)	Impact of event (the effect it had)	What the event triggered next
1.			
2.			
3.			
4.			

Are Haiti and the Philippines risky places to live?

▶ Purpose ◀

The purpose of this enquiry is to investigate the concepts of risk and vulnerability in relation to natural hazards. The pupils begin by asking what makes a place risky? This question is designed to open up responses and acts as a platform for delving deeper into the concepts of risk and vulnerability with increasing complexity. Through this introduction, pupils will be able to consider their own locations and to identify factors that create risk.

Central to this enquiry are the key geographical issues of population growth, rural to urban migration and global disparity. Through examining the concept of 'risky places', pupils will begin to recognise that the causal factors will vary from place to place and that some places are consequently more risky than others. Having built up a conceptual understanding of risk, the pupils progress through the enquiry by developing their analytical skills whilst examining trends in natural disasters.

There are some interesting trends that emerge from the data and pupils are encouraged to spend time looking for and explaining patterns, and linking these to increases in population as well as improved reporting and recording processes. Central to this enquiry is developing a deep understanding of the factors that increase or decrease the vulnerability of people to natural disasters. Initially, pupils are supported in developing an understanding of these factors, before being encouraged to explain how these factors increase or decrease risk and vulnerability.

The enquiry focuses on two places that have suffered significant loss of life, over time and in recent high profile natural disasters – Haiti and the Philippines. Both of these nations illustrate the risks that vulnerable people face from a range of hazards, and pupils are asked to apply their knowledge and understanding to these countries to analyse exactly why people there are more vulnerable. Pupils are then asked to focus on either Haiti or the Philippines – in particular, the Haiti earthquake in 2010 or Typhoon Haiyan in 2013.

Pupils are given opportunities to use GIS within the enquiry. Reducing risk and vulnerability is a key part of the work of the United Nations International Strategy for Disaster Reduction, so the enquiry finishes by introducing the pupils to the Tenorio family, who were tragically impacted upon by the events in the Philippines in 2013. Pupils are supported in developing and making creative products that use appropriate technology to reduce risk and vulnerability. This allows them to demonstrate their knowledge and understanding in an engaging and practical way, and could be the basis for some interesting cross-curricular work with Design, Technology and Science.

▶Aims ◀

Through this enquiry, pupils will be challenged and supported to:

- Develop contextual knowledge of the location of globally significant places, including their defining physical and human geographical characteristics, and how these provide a geographical context for understanding the actions of geographical processes.

- Understand the processes that give rise to key physical and human features of the world, how these are interdependent and how they bring about spatial variation and change over time.

- Interpret a range of sources of geographical information about physical and human processes to reach substantiated conclusions and judgements consistent with the evidence, and communicate these in a variety of ways, including through maps, numerical and quantitative skills and writing at length.

- Reflect on their own worldview of current geographical issues and challenges, and communicate their feelings and ideas appropriately.

▶Links to Key Stage 3 subject content ◀

Pupils should be taught to:

Locational knowledge

- Extend their locational knowledge and deepen their spatial awareness of the world's countries, including the key physical and human characteristics, countries and major cities of Asia.

Place knowledge

- Understand geographical similarities, differences and links between places.

Human and physical geography

- Understand through the use of detailed place-based exemplars at a variety of scales the key processes in:

    o   Physical geography relating to weather and climate and tectonic processes.

    o   Human geography relating to population, urbanisation and international development.

- Understand how human and physical processes interact to influence and change landscapes and environments.

Geographical skills and fieldwork

- Build on their knowledge of globes, maps and atlases, and apply and develop this knowledge routinely in the classroom.

- Interpret topographical and thematic mapping, and aerial and satellite photographs.

- Use Geographical Information Systems (GIS) to view, analyse and interpret places and data.

▶Possible assessable outcomes ◀

- A creative piece of work (video, presentation, poster, etc.) to show understanding of risk and vulnerability in one named location, focusing on a recent natural disaster. Alternatively, the final task could assess pupils by asking them to develop prototypes and create sales pitches in a *Dragons' Den* style.

Question 5.2: Is the world experiencing more disasters?

Use the four graphs featured on the next few pages and the instructions from the Student Book to analyse these graphs.

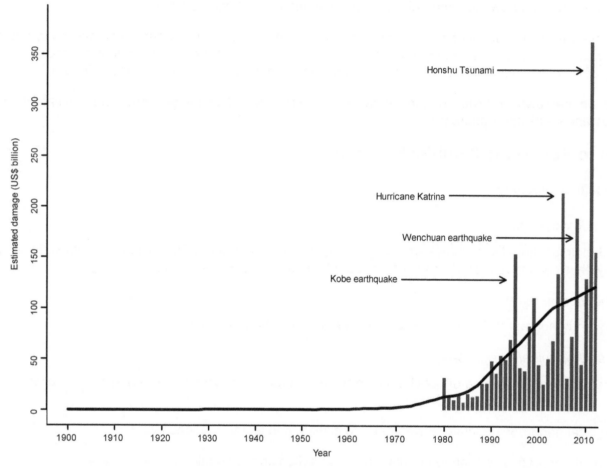

Estimated damage (US$ billion) caused by reported natural disasters 1900 - 2012

EM-DAT: The OFDA/CRED International Disaster Database - www.emdat.be - Université Catholique de Louvain, Brussels - Belgium

_____

_____

_____

_____

_____

_____

_____

_____

_____

Natural disasters reported 1900 - 2013

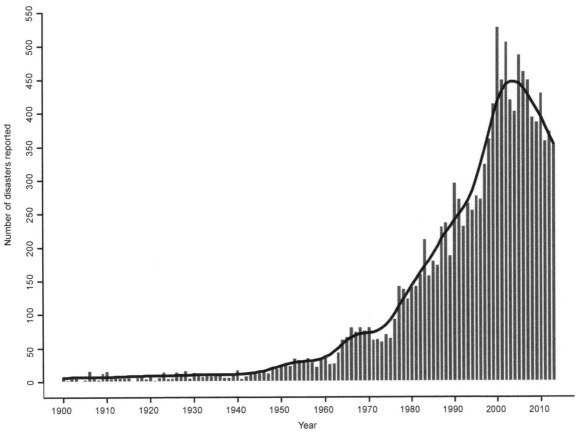

EM-DAT: The OFDA/CRED International Disaster Database - w w w .emdat.be - Université Catholique de Louvain, Brussels - Belgium

_____

_____

_____

_____

_____

_____

_____

_____

_____

_____

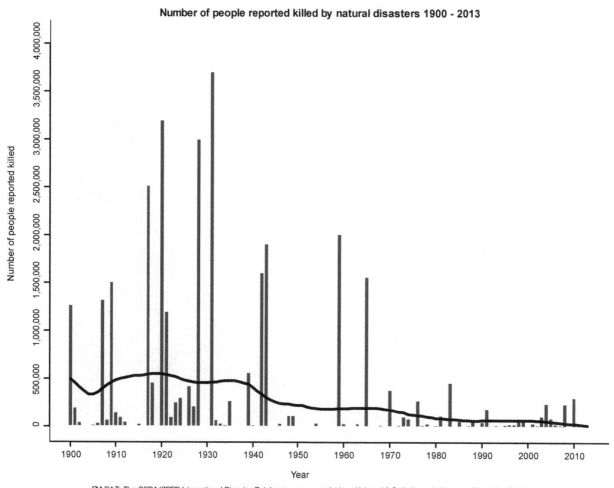

Number of people reported killed by natural disasters 1900 - 2013

EM-DAT: The OFDA/CRED International Disaster Database - www.emdat.be - Université Catholique de Louvain, Brussels - Belgium

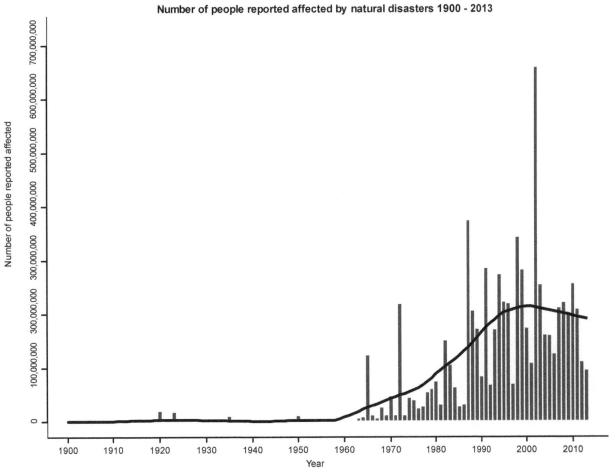

Number of people reported affected by natural disasters 1900 - 2013

EM-DAT: The OFDA/CRED International Disaster Database - w w w .emdat.be - Université Catholique de Louvain, Brussels - Belgium

_____

_____

_____

_____

_____

_____

_____

_____

_____

_____

_____

Disasters and risky places: Question 5.4: Why are the Philippines and Haiti risky places to live?

Range and examples of hazards faced:

Sketch map, including hazards and key geographical features:

Insert two images to illustrate:

Country name and location:

Key geographical facts:

Why do hazards in this country become disasters? (Try to draw together different ideas from this sheet and your research)

Why are the Philippines and Haiti risky places to live?

Group task:

Having completed the research framework and considered why hazards become disasters in these places, you will now need to work with a small group to produce an outcome piece of work that demonstrates your skills, knowledge and understanding of disasters and risky places. This work has to focus on either the Philippines or Haiti.

Your group will have to decide which country to focus on and how you will present your research. You could choose to:

- Design and produce a video news report using an app like iMovie or a programme such as moviemaker

- Construct a presentation using software or apps such as PowerPoint, emaze, or prezi

- Design and produce a large poster

If you have other creative ideas, then discuss these with your teacher. However you choose to present your research, your work must contain the following four sections:

- Background to the country – Location, geographic features, population statistics

- Why is the country at risk? – Focus on all the factors that cause vulnerability of the population and increase risk from disasters

- What happened on... – Focus on a specific disaster event covering:

  o *Causes:* what factors combined to cause the disaster?

  o *Effects:* what effect did the disaster have on people, the economy and the environment?

  o *Response:* how did people, government and aid agencies react to the disaster in the hours, days, weeks, months and years afterwards?

  A clear conclusion that sums up why the country is a risky place to live for some people

The best work will include further research and references to other disaster events the country has experienced. Your work must make use of the information in the Student Book, the supporting material from the Teacher Book and include images, maps, animation and video where appropriate.

Extending your enquiry

You could make use of the 'add image overlay' feature in *Google Earth* to create a hazard map. You can easily create image overlays to show population density, earthquake shake maps, damage maps etc. Ask your teacher for further guidance.

You can also build your own storm track maps (http://csc.noaa.gov/hurricanes/#) and you can search for GIS layers. Try 'Haiti 2010 kml' or 'Typhoon Haiyan crisis map'.

Search for 'Haiti 2010 before and after' and 'Haiti 2010 360 degree street view' or go to http://immersivemedia.com/content/ and look for Philippines Haiyan to take an interactive tour of the disaster zone.

Read about disaster recovery: http://www.theguardian.com/cities/2014/jan/27/port-au-prince-collision-progress-haiti-earthquake

Question 5.5: How can you reduce vulnerability to hazards?

Use the following guidance to persuade people that your product or idea is the most effective:

Remember: Speaker 'Do's

1   Stand up straight. Do not slump, lean, or sway when speaking.

2   Speak slowly and clearly, pronouncing words correctly.

3   Look at the audience. Speakers will be viewed as better informed and more sincere if they make eye contact with the audience.

4   Emphasise main points by letting your voice rise and fall.

5   Use gestures and facial expressions to express an idea and to show enthusiasm for your topic.

6   Use note cards to guide you in speaking.

7   Practise your speech.

8   Be excited and motivated. The audience will 'catch' your enthusiasm.

9   Dress to complement your speech, not to detract from your delivery.

10 Relax, be proud of your accomplishment!

Remember to be persuasive

1   Remember to open with an interesting or shocking start; make it memorable and get their interest!

2   Use rhetorical questions to get people thinking like you.

3   Use plenty of facts that will support your product or argument.

4   Talk about what it could do for the audience and how it could improve their lives.

5   Use a caring, assured voice.

6   Engage the whole audience by giving them plenty of eye contact.

Use the peer assessment grid on the next page to assess the different presentations.

Consider the seven points in the table. Give each group a score out of five for each of the points.

Group name:	1	2	3	4	5
1. Did they grab your interest from the beginning?					
2. Did they back up what they said with facts and statistics?					
3. Did they say why and how this would reduce vulnerability to hazards?					
4. Did they use rhetorical questions effectively?					
5. Did they speak confidently and clearly?					
6. Did they make plenty of eye contact?					
7. Did they ensure that their idea or product was affordable and easy to make?					
Total score:					

6 Don't snatch!

How is so-called 'land grabbing' affecting Africa?

▶Purpose◀

This enquiry enables pupils to investigate a contemporary and relevant geographical issue, which is an emerging feature of the twenty-first century and set to become of increasing significance globally. The roots of 'land grabbing' lie in the days of expanding European empires of the nineteenth century and some people do indeed consider the modern day phenomenon as neo-colonialism. Geography lies at the very core of 'land grabbing' since it exemplifies people–environment relationships and interaction.

Through this investigation, pupils are able to understand what 'land grabbing' is and who the main players currently are, the global patterns of those countries that seek overseas resources and those that sell or lease their resources to others. Through examining the causes of the 'land grabbing' trend, pupils are able to make links to rising world food prices and the increasing consumerism and adoption of more western lifestyles by rapidly developing Asian nations.

The enquiry focuses on the continent of Africa and the country of Ethiopia in particular, where companies from India, China, Saudi Arabia and the UAE have all purchased or leased land from the government.

Towards the end of the enquiry the pupils are encouraged and supported to reflect on the potential costs and benefits of the phenomenon of 'land grabbing', both to 'recipient' and 'donor' countries, and to contribute their own thoughts and perspectives through a piece of discursive writing.

Above all, this enquiry lies at the heart of modern geography since it explores an aspect of global interdependence with very clear economic and cultural perspectives, which is set to be of growing significance during the lifetime of pupils as the twenty-first century unfolds.

▶Aims◀

Through this enquiry, pupils will be challenged and supported to:

- Develop contextual knowledge of the location of globally significant places, including their defining physical and human geographical characteristics, and how these provide a geographical context for understanding the actions of geographical processes.

- Understand the processes that give rise to key physical and human features of the world, how these are interdependent and how they bring about spatial variation and change over time.

- Interpret a range of sources of geographical information about physical and human processes to reach substantiated conclusions and judgements consistent with the evidence, and communicate these in a variety of ways, including through maps, numerical and quantitative skills and writing at length.

- Reflect on their own worldview of current geographical issues and challenges, and communicate their feelings and ideas appropriately.

▶ Links to Key Stage 3 subject content ◀

Pupils should be taught to:

Locational knowledge

- Extend their locational knowledge and deepen their spatial awareness of the world's countries, including the key physical and human characteristics, countries and major cities of Africa.

Place knowledge

- Understand geographical similarities, differences and links between places.

Human and physical geography

- Understand through the use of detailed place-based exemplars at a variety of scales the key processes in:

    o Physical geography relating to weather and climate.

    o Human geography relating to international development, economic activity and the use of natural resources.

- Understand how human and physical processes interact to influence and change landscapes and environments.

Geographical skills and fieldwork

- Build on their knowledge of globes, maps and atlases, and apply and develop this knowledge routinely in the classroom.

- Interpret topographical and thematic mapping, and aerial and satellite photographs.

- Use Geographical Information Systems (GIS) to view, analyse and interpret places and data.

▶ Possible assessable outcomes ◀

- A piece of extended discursive writing, which accurately identifies, describes and explains the phenomenon of 'land grabbing' and evaluates its costs and benefits to the 'donor' countries of Africa and the 'recipient' countries of Asia and the Middle East.

Australia's Long Drought Withering Wheat, Rice Supplies

Carolyn Barry in Sydney, Australia
for National Geographic News

Les Gordon is no stranger to Australia's harsh climate. A rice grower from the country's breadbasket region, some 512 miles (820 kilometres) southwest of Sydney, Gordon has spent almost half his three decades of farming battling drought.

But the most recent dry spell threatens to end his rice-growing days altogether.

'This is the first time we haven't had any rice since my grandfather planted his first crop in 1949,' he said. 'This is the worst drought in a long time.'

In Australia, the world's driest inhabited continent, drought punctuates the climate record with disheartening regularity.

There's not been a decade since official records began that hasn't seen severe rain shortage. Down here drought is just a part of life.

But the onset of two record-breaking droughts in the past seven years – one of them widely considered 'the worst drought in a thousand years' – has had far-reaching and crippling effects.

Major river systems are drying up. The Murray-Darling River Basin – home to 40 percent of Australia's agricultural industry – is at record low levels.

The dearth of water has ravaged Australian agriculture, from wheat to dairy, meat to wine. Some industries will take years to recover.

Rice farmers have arguably fared the worst: Production has been slashed to a measly 2 percent of pre-drought totals. Exports have virtually ceased.

Though Australian rice accounts for less than one percent of the global rice trade, 'normal production levels would feed 40 million people around the world every day,' said Gordon, who is also president of the Rice Growers' Association of Australia.

'Now we'll be able to supply a lot of Australia pretty well, but not much beyond that.'

Australia's weather woes underscore the vulnerability of the world's food production to unexpected natural crises. With reserve food supplies in many countries dwindling as supply outstrips demand, even small drops in production are enough to send prices soaring.

Adding to the concern are predictions that global warming will increase the number and intensity of such unusual climatic events.

Australia will suffer from more frequent droughts, more extreme weather, and less annual rainfall in coming years, according to a recent climate change report by scientists from government agencies, the Commonwealth Scientific and Industrial Research Organization (CSIRO), and the Bureau of Meteorology.

Australian wheat makes up about 15 percent of the grain's world trade, so even small changes can ripple throughout the global market.

Farmers Still Suffering

Despite the inflated grain export prices, 'in the last two to three years a lot of small grain traders have gone broke,' said Peter Wright, a wheat farmer in Cowra, a town 188 miles (300 kilometres) west of Sydney.

Figures from the Australian Bureau of Statistics show that 10,636 families gave up farming during the most severe drought years, between 2001 and 2006.

Profits from the increased prices are often used to pay off debts racked up during the drought or to invest in technology to improve yields and increase water efficiency, Wright added. Record-high costs of fertilizer, fuel, and chemicals also offset export prices.

'We'll need four to five years of high prices to break even,' he said.

Australia's relatively small population of 21 million consumes roughly a third of the country's agricultural products, with the rest sent overseas.

The reliance on world trade means domestic prices often mirror global prices, says Terry Sheales, chief commodity analyst at the Australian Bureau of Agricultural and Resource Economics.

And those inflated prices have filtered down to retailers and consumers.

James Kidman, executive chef at Otto Ristorante, a modern Italian restaurant in inner Sydney, has noticed big increases in the cost of fruits, vegetables, and meat products, especially high-end cuts.

To protect patrons from price hikes, Kidman tries to 'simplify the food,' which means buying less expensive cuts of meat and 'getting creative' negotiating with suppliers. Most other businesses have no choice but to pass on the extra costs to customers.

Back at the farm, average rains are predicted for the coming months and producers are hopeful of a reprieve.

'No drought has gone on forever,' rice farmer Gordon said. 'We'll get our turn eventually.'

The Telegraph

China's changing eating habits

China's economic growth has gone hand in hand with an even more rapid growth in obesity levels.

By Bee Wilson 7 February 2013

Raise the lanterns, it'll soon be Chinese New Year. To mark the date, I'll be cooking a meal. There'll be fish-fragrant aubergines, tenderstem broccoli in ginger sauce, chicken with chestnuts and a mound of steaming rice. To finish, we'll feast on juicy lychees. Whenever I attempt to cook a Chinese meal, however ineptly, it makes me think: the Chinese really know how to eat. From the delicate knife work to the balance of flavours, everything seems so well designed, both for health and pleasure. The greenery and the meat. The spicy and the sweet. The ginger and the garlic. Yin and yang.

But all is not so perfectly balanced in China's eating habits. Their brilliant cooking has not saved the Chinese from catching the obesity of the developed world. The country's economic growth has gone hand in hand with an even more rapid growth in weight. There are now about 100 million obese people in China, five times as many as in 2002. When it comes to obesity-related diseases, China is fast catching up with America. A medical study from 2010 estimated that 9.7 per cent of China's population now has diabetes, as against 11 per cent for America.

What made China fat? The Chinese case resembles a speeded-up version of our own obesity crisis. Cars, city life, television, fast food, a taste for beer and lack of exercise are all factors. The growth of the fast-food market (now worth more than $70 billion) has been dizzying. Fried chicken, burgers and sugary sodas are ubiquitous. At the same time, China's roads, once crowded with bicycles, are jammed with people sitting in cars.

The new rich in China are spending their spare cash on foods that their parents – who lived through the famine of 1958 to 1961 – never knew. Magnums and Whoppers are high-status objects of desire. In the first six years of this millennium chocolate sales quadrupled in China. Cake and cream became a 'concept' for the first time, as French and Crabbe write. Most surprisingly, coffee chains have even persuaded many of these committed tea-drinkers to switch to calorie-laden milky coffee.

You wouldn't think that a great cuisine such as China's could be undermined so quickly in favour of pizza and instant noodles. But the new apartments in which the new young rich live have tiny kitchens, making eating out the more attractive option; and eating Western-style junk still has a cachet. As always in China, the pace of change is terrifying. It is sad to think that, while I cook my faux-Chinese meal to celebrate, millions in China will salute the year of the snake with fries and a shake.

Global food crisis: The challenge of changing diets

Demands for a more western diet in some emerging countries could have a more detrimental affect on global health and hunger than population growth

Why will nearly one in seven people go to bed hungry tonight? After all, the world currently produces enough food for everyone. Today's major problems in the food system are not fundamentally about supply keeping up with demand, but more about how food gets from fields and on to forks.

Hunger – along with obesity, obscene waste and appalling environmental degradation – is an outcome of our broken food system. And the challenge of producing enough food to meet demand looks set to increase. With the world's population expected to grow from around 7 billion today to more than 9 billion in 2050 – an increase of nearly one-third – there will certainly be a lot more stomachs to fill. The UN has forecast that, on current trends, demand may increase by 70% over the same period, and that's without even tackling current levels of hunger.

But population growth, per se, is not the primary problem. By 2050 an estimated seven out of 10 people will live in poor countries reliant on food imports. The quantities of food eaten by each of these people every day is likely to be an unjustifiable fraction of what anyone reading this blog has already eaten today.

Instead, the real crunch is likely to come from the changing dietary preferences from people in some large emerging countries. Economic growth, urbanisation and rising affluence are increasingly bringing with them higher demand for convenient, processed foods, for meat, and for dairy products – in short, a more western diet.

This change in demand has significant environmental consequences. Feeding livestock is much less resource-efficient than growing grains for human consumption. Already, one-third of the world's cereal harvest and more than nine-tenths of the world's soya is used for animal feed. Soy-derived feed may be produced on, or indirectly contribute to expansion on to, cleared rainforest land. Rainforests are very important natural carbon sinks and therefore their clearance accelerates climate change, which is already challenging food production the world over.

The production of 1kg of beef uses 12 times the amount of water needed to produce 1kg of wheat, and more than five times the amount of land.

Changing diets bring significant social challenges. Malnourishment in the form of over-eating as well as under-eating will increasingly clog up healthcare systems and arteries in the developing world. In the rich world, obesity afflicts the poorer segments of society, because healthy foods are frequently more expensive. In the US, seven of the 10 states with the highest poverty levels are also among the 10 states with the highest rates of obesity. But in emerging countries obesity tends to be concentrated in the middle classes – those who lead more sedentary lifestyles and consume more processed foods. Countries such as Mexico and South Africa are having to increasingly deal with problems of the over-fed at the same time as those of the under-fed.

But before we point the finger at emerging economies for their rising consumption, let's keep things in perspective. In 2007, the average American ate more than twice as much meat as the average Chinese resident. At the same time, consumers in rich countries waste almost as much food as the entire food production of sub-Saharan Africa. So while rising affluence and changing diets are certainly set to pose some challenges over the coming years, we should perhaps start by looking long and hard at the contents of own fridges and dustbins.

Richard King Policy Research Advisor, Oxfam GB

Discursive writing aims to present a balanced argument, usually about a controversial issue, and often answers a question.

Audience

Will usually be people who need to be 'briefed' about an issue that they currently don't know much about and advised as to the best way forward.

Purpose

Is normally to present arguments and information from different viewpoints and suggest a solution.

Text level features

Title: Will often be a question or statement.

Introduction

The introduction is very important in a discursive piece of writing, such as a report, as it presents the subject, provides the background to the issue, defines important terms and captures the attention of the reader, encouraging them to read on.

Main body

Alternate paragraphs showing different sides of an argument, introduced with a topic sentence that is then developed, drawing upon evidence such as comments of individuals, statistics, photographs and diagrams to support a point of view.

Conclusion

Summarises arguments and gives the writer's own view and recommendations.

Sentence level features

- Always written in third person (*he, she, they*) to make the writing impersonal and formal although the writer might use the first person (*I*) when they are presenting their own opinions and recommendations.

- Usually written in the present tense.

- The writer will use connectives – words and devices that signal a move or link from one side of an argument to the other – which helps the writing flow as one continuous piece, despite presenting different arguments. Connectives are most often used at the beginning of paragraphs and sentences but can also link ideas within a sentence. Examples that help to develop the same line of thought include 'secondly', 'etc.', 'next',

'furthermore', 'likewise', 'for instance', 'for example', 'so that', 'accordingly', 'in addition', and 'similarly'. In a conclusion or summary a writer may use 'thus', 'therefore', 'consequently', 'despite the fact that', 'in retrospect', 'hence', 'in conclusion', 'the result of this is', and 'to sum up'. Words and phrases such as 'without question', 'without doubt', 'unquestionably', 'despite the fact that…' are used to help make definite statements. To introduce a contrasting idea or point of view a writer might use 'yet', 'on the other hand', 'nevertheless', 'however', 'conversely', 'in contrast to', 'in addition', 'another point to consider is…', 'there is also the fact that…' and 'moreover'.

- Words and devices showing cause and effect are often used to argue a particular case, e.g. 'therefore', 'consequently', 'this means that'.

- The writer will usually use generalised nouns such as 'residents', 'conservationists', 'planners', 'developers', 'the public', etc.

- Many of the sentences may be statements but the writer may use rhetorical questions for effect such as 'Is this true? We need to balance the evidence with…'

Word level features

The writer may use emotive words and phrases to describe strong opinions and views, e.g. 'scandal', 'abandoned', 'betrayed', 'disaster', 'stupendous', 'world class', 'irreplaceable'.

Formal tone in a discursive piece of writing

It is important when writing a discursive piece to write in a formal way. In simple terms this means the following:

Do

- Write in proper and complete sentences

- Use complete words and expressions

- Use proper standard English

Do not use

- Abbreviations such as 'i.e.', 'e.g.', 'etc.', 'UK', '&'

- Slang such as 'bloke'

- Colloquial language such as 'mate', 'bolshy', etc.

What should happen to Amazonia?

Report to the International Committee of Friends of the Earth

Title summating topic

Purpose and audience

Without a doubt the future of the human race depends on having thriving forests around the world and none is as critical as Amazonia. It is not over dramatic to say that if we lose forests such as Amazonia then we all take one giant step closer to extinction as a species. Why is this? Firstly, Amazonia is home to thousands of species of wild animals and plants, some of which have never been identified, let alone studied seriously. Secondly, the roots of the trees bind the soil together and help prevent soil erosion. Once the soil is exposed to heavy rain then the process of desertification gets under way and before long only barren scrub remains where once majestic trees towered into the sky. Furthermore, fewer trees in the Amazonian forest will mean less rain, not only for Brazil, but for the world as a whole. However, there is another side to the story of disappearing Amazonia. For example, it's very easy, from the comfort of armchairs in privileged western homes, to overlook the reality of life for tens of millions of people who attempt to survive on a day-to-day basis in Amazonia. In contrast to our electrified and centrally heated world, their only source of heat and light and perhaps a meagre income from selling timber, is the forest that surrounds them. So, there are two points of view to bear in mind when considering the future of Amazonian forests: should we protect the forests or allow them to be cut down?

Emotive words

Introductory paragraph to show the topic under discussion

Connective

Connective

Those who support the continued logging of forests emphasise that the world needs wood for all kinds of products as well as very basic requirements such as building shelters in which to live. What exactly are these terribly poor people in places such as Brazil supposed to do if they can't cut the trees down? So another very important point to consider in all of this is the fact that banning the felling of trees will sentence fellow human beings in Amazonia to a miserable existence for the rest of their lives. As one forester put it to a visiting conservationist 'for us, trees are life'. There is no chance either that all of the people currently living in Amazonia could realistically move somewhere else in order to 'save' the forest. For example, countries neighbouring Brazil have made it abundantly clear that they will not, under any circumstances, allow in any refugees who can no longer survive in Amazonia. Let's be honest with ourselves, would they be welcome in Britain?

Rhetorical question

Comments

Connective

Rhetorical question

Example of discursive writing

Connective

Statistics

On the other hand, conservationists point out that an area of Amazonia the size of Wales (21,000 km²) is cut down every year, destroying forever rare plants and endangering animals. Another point to consider is that scientists are afraid that plant species that could provide the key to curing diseases such as cancer will be lost for ever. Can we really afford to do this? Furthermore, as Amazonia is cut down, the soil on the mountain sides is loosened. This can literally be an absolute disaster. Heavy rain then washes it downhill into the rivers in lowland areas.

General noun

Cause and effect

This means that as the rivers are made shallower by silt, they flood more often and more seriously, ruining crops in the valleys and washing people and property away. Most devastating of all, scientists say, is the potential impact of losing Amazonia on global climate change. Fewer trees means more carbon dioxide in the atmosphere. In turn, more carbon dioxide means an increasing likelihood of a warmer atmosphere and devastating climate change.

General noun

Connective

In conclusion, this seems to be an impossible problem to solve. If we ban the felling of trees in Amazonia then we will condemn millions of people to misery and quite possibly a horrible death. On the other hand if we allow the wholesale destruction of the forests the ecological and environmental impact will be disastrous. But maybe there's another way? I believe that with careful planning and monitoring there is a compromise position that both the people who live in Amazonia and conservationists will find acceptable. Trees are after all a renewable resource: trees that are cut down can be replaced with new ones given time. This kind of sustainable management (cut one, plant one) would mean that in the long term the area of Amazonia would remain the same. The most precious areas could be designated national nature reserves in which there would never be any logging. Less important parts of Amazonia could be put aside for carefully planned cutting and replanting with an annual limit to the number of trees that can be cut. This would require the residents of the forest to be educated of course (most are illiterate and suspicious of outsiders) about the importance of sustainable development and to be provided with young saplings to plant by their government. I'm not saying it will be easy and that there won't be setbacks from time to time but it is what I would recommend. The result of this would be to maintain a balance between the immediate needs of the people of the Amazonia and the long term needs of nature and the health of the planet. When it comes down to it, do we really have a choice?

Summary of points of view

First person to present personal opinion

Present tense

Emotive word

First person

Recommendation

Rhetorical question

The area of land affected by so-called 'land grabbing' is tiny. Less than 1% of the world's total farmland and only 3% of the arable land of Ethiopia.

It is morally and ethically wrong for one country to own and control the natural resources of another country.

There are millions of hectares of potentially fertile land in Africa owned at the moment by countries that will never be able to afford to modernise them. So why not let someone else do it?

In many parts of Africa the land is not suited to modern, hi-tech agribusiness, which leads to environmental problems such as soil erosion.

The governments of African countries receive big payments in exchange for the land they sell and lease. This can be used to improve the lives of local people by building hospitals and schools.

Local people who are uprooted from the land that their families have farmed for generations not only lose their source of livelihood but also their sense of social and cultural identity.

Local people who have to leave their lands are almost always compensated financially for their loss.

The new agribusiness farm estates run by foreign companies create paid work for local people in some of the poorest parts of Africa where money is desperately needed.

Once the new and very efficient agribusiness operations are up and running, the price of food products locally often drops. This means that local small-scale farmers cannot compete and so they receive less and less income.

Only companies based in richer developed countries outside of Africa can afford the investment needed to transform millions of hectares of under-used land in Africa into productive farms.

Some of the land acquired by foreign companies is not farmland at all, but forest, which is then cut down and burned, creating serious environmental problems such as local droughts and the release of greenhouse gases.

As a result of the arrival of foreign agribusinesses, Ethiopia now exports US$60 million of fruit and vegetables and US$160 million of flowers every year.

By 2075 the world's population will rise by 2 billion to 9.2 billion and opening up the underdeveloped lands of Africa is an important way of ensuring that these extra people are fed.

In Ethiopia the high-tech production of sesame, an oilseed grown by Chinese companies for chocolates and biscuits, has already driven down the price that small-scale farmers receive for their sesame.

Few displaced locals who get jobs in the commercial farms have a contract or are paid more than the minimum subsistence wage.

Most of the farmland bought or leased by foreign companies in Ethiopia is the poorer lowland with a harsh climate and malaria infestation, which local people tend to avoid anyway.

Foreign companies who set up commercial farms develop infrastructure such as roads, railways and electricity supplies, which benefit the whole country, not just themselves.

Modern agribusiness farms require huge amounts of irrigation water, which leads to the drying up of local streams and lakes on which local people depend for drinking water.

Human rights observers have witnessed examples of local people being forcibly driven off their ancestral lands so that it can be sold by the government.

The resentment created by forced removals to inferior quality marginal land with poorer services has led to demonstrations and the fear of rioting in some African countries.

7 Olympic spirit

Where should the 2022 Winter Olympics be held?

▶Purpose◀

This investigation is designed to enable pupils to explore the relationship between the physical environment and human activity and to make real-life decisions given a range of evidence and information. By using the Winter Olympics, an event which the pupils may have followed and have some prior knowledge of, they are introduced to the different factors which the International Olympic Committee (IOC) take into consideration to make their decision as to who should be given the honour of hosting. Factors such as a suitable climate for winter sports are fairly obvious but there are a number of other considerations, such as local support, positive media coverage and enough hotel rooms to house the athletes, journalists and tourists, which are also important. Having a large enough budget to stage the Games successfully is vital; Sochi 2014 was the most expensive Olympics (either summer or winter) ever staged, costing the Russians US$51 billion.

Pupils are asked to consider the advantages of spending so much money and to classify them. Ways of classifying are suggested (although pupils could suggest another method) and can be used individually or combined to differentiate this task. The five contenders for the 2022 Winter Olympics are then introduced and pupils are encouraged to carry out a decision-making exercise using materials from the Teacher Book.

It is important for pupils to understand that there is no one 'correct' answer and different people may reach different conclusions given the same evidence. The main thing is that pupils can justify their opinions and support these with factual data. The pupils can then write up their findings in an extended piece of persuasive writing. An example of this task is given in the Teacher Book. It is not intended to be a model answer. It has been left deliberately undeveloped as critiquing it forms part of the pupils' investigation. Whilst the author makes a range of sensible points and is fairly persuasive, the writing lacks detail, factual support of the points and powerful language.

The enquiry can then be extended in three separate ways. Firstly, pupils can consider whether a southern hemisphere country would make a good contender as host of the Winter Olympics in the future. Secondly, the environmental impact of winter sports, particularly skiing, is explored. Finally, pupils are asked to assess the environmental impact and sustainability of the Sochi Winter Olympics and to suggest ways in which the 2022 host could be as sustainable as possible.

▶ Aims ◀

Through this enquiry, pupils will be challenged and supported to:

- Develop contextual knowledge of the location of globally significant places, including their defining physical and human geographical characteristics, and how these provide a geographical context for understanding the actions of geographical processes.

- Understand the processes that give rise to key physical and human features of the world, how these are interdependent and how they bring about spatial variation and change over time.

- Interpret a range of sources of geographical information to reach substantiated conclusions and judgements consistent with the evidence, and communicate these in a variety of ways, including through maps, numerical and quantitative skills and writing at length.

▶ Links to Key Stage 3 subject content ◀

Pupils should be taught to:

Locational knowledge

- Extend their locational knowledge and deepen their spatial awareness of the world's countries, including the key physical and human characteristics and major cities of those in Russia and Asia.

Human and physical geography

- Understand through the use of detailed place-based exemplars at a variety of scales the key processes in physical geography relating to weather and climate and glaciation.

- Understand how human and physical processes interact to influence and change landscapes, environments and the climate and how human activity relies on effective functioning of natural systems.

Geographical skills and fieldwork

- Build on their knowledge of globes, maps and atlases, and apply and develop this knowledge routinely in the classroom.

- Interpret topographical and thematic mapping, and aerial and satellite photographs.

▶ Possible assessable outcomes ◀

- A piece of extended persuasive writing which puts forward a justification for one of five shortlisted host cities of the 2022 Winter Olympics. The piece should explain why the city should be chosen as well as why the others are not as suitable.

- A website home-page for the city which has been chosen to host the 2022 Winter Olympics. The page will welcome visitors and give information about the city. The home-page should feature an introduction to the city, a map and a description of its location. Images to show what the city is like and factual information should also be included.

- A poster which promotes one of three possible southern hemisphere cities which have the potential to hold the Winter Olympics in the future. This should include a logo, a slogan and at least three reasons why it would be a suitable venue.

In order to decide which city should host the 2022 Winter Olympics, you will need to carry out some research. The table below will help you to structure your research.

In the left hand column of the table are some of the factors which the IOC will take into account when making their decision. Once you have filled in the tables you can think of a couple of your own factors and create a similar table if you want to.

The middle column contains the names of the five potential host cities for each of the factors. You need to research information using the weblinks below to determine how suitable each city is. See the example below to help you think about the sort of thing you need to write:

Factor	Comment	Rank
Climate	Krakow, Poland: –2 °C and 34 mm of precipitation in February. Climate is suitable for winter sports as precipitation may fall as snow as it is below freezing.	
	Oslo, Norway: –4 °C and 21 cm of snow in February.	
	Almaty, Kazakhstan:	
	Lviv, Ukraine:	
	Beijing, China:	

Weblinks to help with your research

General websites

- http://en.wikipedia.org/wiki/2022_Winter_Olympics

- http://www.olympic.org/content/the-ioc/bidding-for-the-games/current-bid-process-2022/

- http://www.gamesbids.com/eng/winter_olympic_bids/index.1.html

Krakow, Poland

- http://en.wikipedia.org/wiki/Krak%C3%B3w_bid_for_the_2022_Winter_Olympics

Oslo, Norway

- http://en.wikipedia.org/wiki/Oslo_bid_for_the_2022_Winter_Olympics

Almaty, Kazakhstan

- http://en.wikipedia.org/wiki/Almaty_bid_for_the_2022_Winter_Olympics

Lviv, Ukraine

- http://en.wikipedia.org/wiki/Lviv_bid_for_the_2022_Winter_Olympics

- http://www.bbc.co.uk/news/world-europe-15983012

Beijing, China

- http://en.wikipedia.org/wiki/Beijing_bid_for_the_2022_Winter_Olympics

- http://www.bbc.co.uk/news/world-asia-china-26478452

- http://www.bbc.co.uk/news/world-asia-26252516

Which city should host the 2022 Winter Olympics?

Factor	Comment	Rank
Climate	Krakow, Poland:	
	Oslo, Norway:	
	Almaty, Kazakhstan:	
	Lviv, Ukraine:	
	Beijing, China:	
Winter sports	Krakow, Poland:	
	Oslo, Norway:	
	Almaty, Kazakhstan:	
	Lviv, Ukraine:	
	Beijing, China:	
Economic development	Krakow, Poland:	
	Oslo, Norway:	
	Almaty, Kazakhstan:	
	Lviv, Ukraine:	
	Beijing, China:	
Transport	Krakow, Poland:	
	Oslo, Norway:	
	Almaty, Kazakhstan:	
	Lviv, Ukraine:	
	Beijing, China:	

Which city should host the 2022 Winter Olympics?

Factor	Comment	Rank
Previous success at managing large sporting events	Krakow, Poland:	
	Oslo, Norway:	
	Almaty, Kazakhstan:	
	Lviv, Ukraine:	
	Beijing, China:	
Local support	Krakow, Poland:	
	Oslo, Norway:	
	Almaty, Kazakhstan:	
	Lviv, Ukraine:	
	Beijing, China:	
Previous hosting	Krakow, Poland:	
	Oslo, Norway:	
	Almaty, Kazakhstan:	
	Lviv, Ukraine:	
	Beijing, China:	
Positive media coverage	Krakow, Poland:	
	Oslo, Norway:	
	Almaty, Kazakhstan:	
	Lviv, Ukraine:	
	Beijing, China:	

Once you have discovered the information for each of the factors and each of the host cities, you need to rank them. Award 1st place to the city that you think is most suitable, down to 5th place for the city that you think is least suitable. Do this for each of the factors.

You then need to add up all the ranks for each of the cities. So, for example, if Krakow, Poland, is ranked 1st, 4th and 5th in three different factors you would add 1 + 4 + 5 = 10 to give a total score of 10. Do this for all five shortlisted cities and all of the factors in the table below. The city with the lowest score is the one which should host the 2022 Winter Olympics.

City ranks for all of the factors	Total score
Krakow, Poland:	
Oslo, Norway:	
Almaty, Kazakhstan:	
Lviv, Ukraine:	
Beijing, China:	

The city with the lowest score, and therefore the one which I think should host the 2022 Winter Olympic Games, is:

Having decided upon the host city for the 2022 Winter Olympics, you have been asked to produce a website home page which welcomes people to the city and promotes it to a wider audience.

You will need to make sure that your website contains the following features:

- An introduction describing what the city is like

- A map and a description of the location of the city

- A range of images to show what the city is like

- Factual information to support your description

Think about the sort of information that would be useful to promote your city. You might want to consider the culture, economy, environment or services that your city has. What makes your city unique? You could design a logo, a motto or slogan to publicise your city and put on the home page.

You can create actual webpages, such as the example below, for free using websites such as www.weebly.com.

Where should the 2022 Winter Olympics be held?

Paragraph 1: Introductory paragraph

The Winter Olympics are held every four years. The last event was in 2014 and was in Sochi which is in Russia. They have already decided who is going to host the 2018 Winter Olympics and it is going to be held in PeongChang which is in South Korea. The city which is going to host the 2022 Winter Olympics has not been decided yet. There are five cities to choose from which are Krakow in Poland, Oslo in Norway, Almaty in Kazakhstan, Lviv in Ukraine and Beijing in China. Looking at all of the evidence, I think Oslo should be the place where the 2022 Winter Olympics are held.

Paragraph 2: Why should my chosen city be the host?

Oslo is the perfect place to hold the Winter Olympics because it has the perfect climate for all of the winter sports. It is below freezing which means that it will probably snow during the event which is important because the competitors need fresh snow to ski and snowboard on. Norway has also hosted the Winter Olympics in the past. This is a massive advantage because they know the sorts of things which will make the Games successful and they have already built some of the venues. Norway has also got a very good transportation system and Oslo has an international airport nearby so people will be able to travel to the Games easily. Also, Norway is an economically developed country and so they will find it quite easy to raise the US$5 billion which is what the Winter Olympics will cost. Norway is also quite a peaceful country and the media coverage is good.

Paragraph 3: Why are the other cities not as suitable?

The other four cities are not as suitable as Oslo in my opinion. Krakow has a good climate and has hosted large winter sports events in the past but has never held a Winter Olympics. Also, the transport system is not as good as Oslo's, although they say that they will redevelop it for the Games. Almaty is also not the best candidate as the 2014 and 2018 Games will be in the same part of the world (Russia and Asia) so it does not seem very fair for them to host three times in a row. Also Kazakhstan is not a very rich country so they might struggle to pay for all of the improvements which are needed. Lviv would have had a good chance but Ukraine is in the news at the moment as there is a lot of unrest in the country and so I don't think this is a good place to have such an important event. Finally, Beijing isn't a very good candidate as there has not been a lot of snowfall in the area and also the pollution levels are very high which will not be good for the athletes.

Paragraph 4: Concluding paragraph

In conclusion, I have decided that Oslo should host the Winter Olympics in 2022 because they have more positives than the other four cities and I think the people of Norway would make it a huge success.

The Sochi Winter Olympics has resulted in a range of positive economic, social and environmental changes. The Sochi sustainability report explores some of these changes and a summary of the report is provided below.

Economic changes

- The Krasnodar region (in which Sochi is located) has seen the multiplier effect working to increase business, create new jobs and develop transport infrastructure.

- Between 2008 and 2010, the number of contractors working in the region doubled and the number of different jobs increased making the economy more diverse.

- Many of the businesses benefitting from the Winter Olympics were not large, global companies but were small businesses and individuals. Their share of the economy increased from 18% in 2008 to 31% in 2011.

- The Krasnodar region has moved up the Russian economy rankings from 27th in 2005 to 14th in 2011.

- The total amount spent on sports facilities and infrastructure by the end of 2012 was US$3.2 billion.

- The Russian government spent almost five times more than this (nearly US$16.5 billion) developing transport, health and social services, tourism facilities and housing in the Sochi area.

- The government lengthened the Tuapse–Adler–Abkhazia railway which runs through the city of Sochi. They also laid more than 1300 km of roads and developed 46 km of footpaths.

- Before the development of the resort, Sochi was a 'summer only' resort and tourism was seasonal. Now, the development of winter sports has reduced the seasonality of tourism.

- The number of tourists increased from three to five million between 2005 and 2009. However, this figure has stagnated and then declined in recent years so that 2011 figures are back to those seen in 2006.

- The city of Sochi has a positive image in the media; negative stories were five times less frequent than positive stories between 2009 and 2010.

- Between 2009 and 2011, the number of international events in Sochi and the surrounding region increased by about 70%. Unsurprisingly, the vast majority of these were sporting events.

- In 2009, the number of jobs increased by more than sixty times compared to 2008 figures. In 2011, approximately 56,000 people were employed working on the Olympic sites.

- Taking into account the multiplier effect, the total number of jobs created by the Olympics is over 560,000.

- In 2011, the unemployment rate was 0.6% lower than the Russian national average.

Social changes

- Between 2005 and 2011, the birth rate in Sochi and the surrounding region grew whilst the death rate fell. Since 2010, the birth rate has been higher than the death rate.

- Sochi has also seen significant population growth due to migration which is thirteen times greater than Russia as a whole.

- In 2010, the Krasnodar region was above average in terms of calorie consumption compared to Russia as a whole (2650 calories per day).

- Housing in Sochi has become more affordable. All of the districts in the city (except Centralny) are dominated by traditional, rural settlements which have their own planning.

- Between 2005 and 2011, the number of people playing sport in Sochi has doubled. The number of women and those with a disability who are playing sport is increasing at a faster rate than the total growth.

- People have become particularly interested in winter sports, especially alpine skiing, snowboarding, figure skating and ice hockey.

- In 2010, Russia's bid to host the 2018 Football World Cup was approved by FIFA and Sochi has been named as one of the host cities. Also, the Russian Grand Prix (based in Sochi) has been added to the Formula 1 calendar and Sochi will be involved in hosting the Ice Hockey World Championships in 2016.

- The Sochi Winter Olympics was the twelfth tobacco-free Games. 80% of people living in Sochi approve of the initiatives to reduce smoking in the city.

- There have been significant changes in attitude to people with a disability. Sochi University has trained thirty-one people to work with people with disabilities and all sports venues are 'barrier free' to make them accessible.

- The percentage of people in Sochi who have a Higher Education is 31%, an increase of 5% since 2002. This is significantly higher than the region of Krasnodar and Russia as a whole.

- The total number of people attending Olympics-based education programmes was over 209,000 people.

- Sochi hosted the Cultural Olympiad between 2010 and 2014 with about 35,000 people visiting concerts, art competitions, festivals and exhibitions.

- Over 25,000 volunteers were working at the Olympics and it is hoped that a culture of volunteering will be one of the legacies of the Games.

Environmental Protection

- There has been a reduction in water consumption, both overall and per person, and water quality has improved slightly.

- There are thirty-four sewerage treatment plants in the city and these are being improved and modernised as part of the redevelopment.

- The concentrations of pollutants, including carbon monoxide, sulphur dioxide and nitrogen oxide, have increased although this is likely to be due to the increased construction work in the city.

- The Olympic buildings are being built to strict environmental standards and include paying attention to the impact on agricultural land and animal habitats, trying to use pre-existing buildings and brownfield sites, developing public transport to reduce greenhouse gases and maximising open spaces.

Read the summary and the full report (using the link provided) and write a conclusion which summarises the main points and makes a statement about how sustainable the Sochi Olympics have been.

Which change do you think has had the most positive effect and why? What do you think the world has learned from the Sochi Winter Olympics? Justify and explain your answers.

You can access the full report at:
http://sochi2014.blob.core.windows.net/storage/games/strategy/OGI_Digest_Eng_fin.pdf

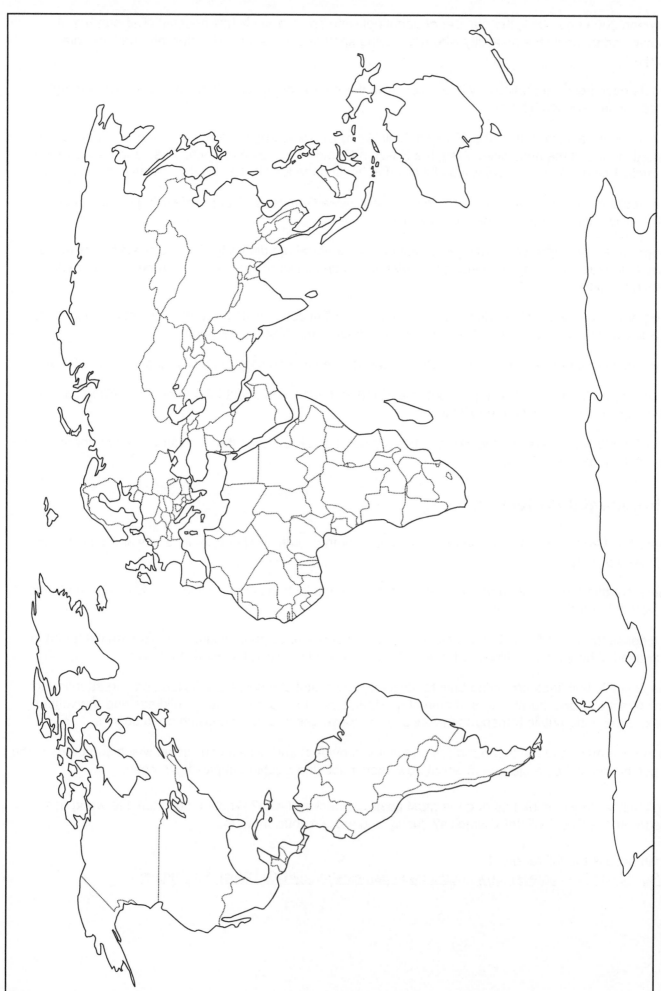

Teachers: add instructions for your own use.

Teachers: add instructions for your own use.

Teachers: add instructions for your own use.

Teachers: add instructions for your own use.

Teachers: add instructions for your own use.